Break From The System

Perspectives On How We Do Church

A Framework For Reformation

Susan, God Bless you & You are already living this life but let me know your thoughts! ♡ Sara

Copyright © 2018 Kenneth E. Purcell

All rights reserved.

ISBN-13: 978-544662947
ISBN-10: 544662947

Break From The System

Perspectives On How We Do Church

A Framework For Reformation

Kenneth E. Purcell

CONTENTS

Chapter 1. Form And Function 1
Humility 3
The Goal 5
The Form 7
The Function 11

Chapter 2. A Disabled Body 14

Chapter 3. To Tithe Or Not To Tithe 16
What Does The New Testament Say About Tithing? 27
What About Abraham And The Tithe? 36
The Bottom Line 41

Chapter 4. The Pastors Place 43
What Is A Pastor? 44
What Is The Function Of A Pastor? 53
Is The Pastor The Only One Qualified To Speak? 61
Should A Pastor Be Paid A Salary? 63

Chapter 5. The Challenge 69
Jesus Did What? 69
The Apostles Did What? 71
What Should We Do? 79
How Do We Get From Where We Are To Where They Were? 83

Chapter 6. A Bell, A Pomegranate, And The Church . .92

Conclusion 97

Acknowledgments

This project would not have been possible without the support of my amazing family. The encouragement and input from my wife Wendy, the advice and help from my sons David and Stephen kept me focused and on track to accomplish the task set before me. A special thank you to Lauren Mathews for her help in the process.

References

Unless otherwise noted all scripture references are from the King James Version. It is in the public domain. KJV

NASB - New American Standard.
Copyright 1960,1962,1963,1968,1971,1973,1975,1977,1995
The Lockman Foundation. Lahabra,Ca. 90631

AMP – The Amplified Version. Copyright 2015
The Lockman Foundation. Lahabra,Ca. 90631

J.B. Phillips New Testament. Copyright 1960,1972
Administered by the Archbishops
Council of the Church of England

NKJV – New King James Version. Copyright 1982.
Thomas Nelson/Harper Collins Publishing
Nashville, TN 37214

TLB – The Living Bible. Copyright 1971.
Tyndale House Publishers Inc.
Carol Stream, IL 60188

NIV – New International Version. Copyright 1973,1978,1984,2011
Biblica Inc/Harper Collins Publishing
Nashville,TN 37214

Kenneth S. Wuest – The New Testament. Copyright 1961
Wm. B. Eardsman Publishing Co.
Grand Rapids, Michigan 49505 Cambridge,UK

Christianity Today Founded 1956
465 Gunderson Drive
Carol Stream, IL 60188

Greek word definitions. Strong's Exhaustive Concordance copyright 2001 Zondervan Publishing. Grand Rapids,MI 49505

Introduction

I was raised Roman Catholic. Even in my youth, I recognized the church should offer more than a basic understanding of God. At the age of seventeen, I experienced a supernatural encounter with God. I felt overwhelmed by an immense enveloping love. I heard what is often referred to as the audible voice of God. I looked around, yet no one was there. The voice was masculine in tone as expected by most, however it was also warm, loving and peaceful. It seemed to permeate the entire room. Desiring to understand God on a deeper level, I engaged this voice in conversation. As God spoke to me, waves of love and peace flowed through my entire being. It was like spiritual water filling me from the inside, and then pouring out into my surroundings. This same voice was known as the voice of many waters as described by the Apostle John in Revelation 14:12. The prophet Ezekiel used the very same description in Ezekiel 43:2. Moses also experienced the audible voice of God as told in the story of the burning bush. (Exodus 3:1-12)

I knew that this experience was a taste of God's boundless glory and holy nature. It was in that moment of basking in the radiant love of God that I became fully aware that Jesus was, is, and will always be the eternal King, who desires to reign in the hearts of all people. Along with this, was the impression that my heart will always be knit together with His. I always understood the concept of God, but now I perceived Him in a very deep and personal way. That night was when I began my journey, a new life of faith. God began to change me from the inside out as I grew in the grace and knowledge of Jesus. I met many wonderful people of faith who helped me on this journey. I encountered many who were free spirited and intuitive. I met some who loved without limits, and others who were religious, dogmatic and judgmental. I encountered similar dynamics in the various church structures where all these people would gather together.

After all this, that same intuitive knowledge I had in my youth was reaffirmed. I passionately felt that there must be a better way to do church.

I do not claim to have all the answers. I simply offer concepts that will revolutionize the way we do church. Church should be about gathering together to experience God in a way that will transform us. The goal is to hear God's voice, to feel his heart and to experience the supernatural presence of God with others. The church has often relegated itself to become a business, with a pastor as its CEO. We need to remember once again how to be a family of God (Ephesians 2:19). A family where each individual can express themselves fully and freely while maintaining peace and order. Jesus said it well when He said Our Father who is in heaven; a family should have structure, but the real value within is relational. The family is made up of individuals who are living epistles of the Grace of God. Yet all too often this family becomes entangled in and bogged down by a religious system.

The system's rules have become unchangeable, the policies have gathered precedence over relationships, and only those that have certification have their voices heard. The pastor, who should be accessible, is often not. The sermon has become the main focal point of the church service and a church often requires people to give ten percent of their income, volunteer, and sign a membership covenant agreement in order to be a full member and do any kind of ministry. Well, for some it may be time to break from the system.

Chapter 1

Form And Function

The church has many labels such as: Christians, believers and the body of Christ. Despite which label is used, the church is always comprised of people. It should *not* be the building that defines it, nor the organizational structure within. It is designed to be a living, breathing organism. The church body ought to be full of life, and build itself up in love and harmony.

There are more than seven billion people living on earth today. There is tremendous diversity within that population. Each person is unique in form and identity. The Apostle Paul used the human body as a way to illustrate the **form** and **function** of this large group of people called the church.

First Corinthians 12:12, "For as the **body** is one and has many members, and all the members of that one body, being many, are one body." Verse 21 says: "And the eye cannot say to the hand, I have no need of you."

I would like to delve even further into the illustration of comparing the church body to the human body. The human body is comprised of cells, and while scientists cannot tell the exact number, there could be as many as thirty seven trillion cells.

Each one having an important role and function. God himself knows the function of each and every cell. Just think about how immense that is. **Each one has a function**. When a body is healthy they all work together in concert like a sweet symphony.

The Apostle Paul had some insight as to this mystery and wonder called the *body of Christ*. Paul compared it to the human body and further stated that there should be no schism in the body. It becomes clear if one takes an honest look at the church body at large today that the body of Jesus has many schisms within it. To some this may seem like magnifying the problem but consider how a doctor or surgeon repairs the human body. They diagnose the problem, examine it closely, identify it, and attempt to find a cure.

We therefore can deduce that God knows each member of the body and the *function* of each one. In the human body members are interdependent on each other, while in the church body we have systems in place that create categories for the members that separate us. Clergy and parishioners, pastors and church members, committed and not committed, those who tithe and those who do not tithe, those who have faith and those who lack faith, those who are sold out and those who are not. The list is long. The ugly truth is we have inadvertently created a cast system within the church.

We have adopted a system of religious hierarchy that self-perpetuates that class system. A psychologist might refer to the current state of the body of Christ as having a split personality. We need to find a way to make the body whole again.

Life can teach us many things. All we need to do is take time to notice what the lesson is and how to apply it. Late in my forties I began to have severe migraine headaches. I was sent to a neurologist who diagnosed a pinched nerve in the neck. A dear friend recommended I try chiropractic treatments. The chiropractor was able to free up the two vertebrae in my neck that were stuck. The end result of the adjustments was complete relief from migraines. This can help us with our view of the church. Jesus is the head. We are the body. It should be evident to most that a **series of adjustments** to the structure of the church body will help the entire body function better, work together easier and overall become healthier. Wholeness is the goal. Thus, I present a series of adjustments that I hope you will consider.

HUMILITY

The first place to start would be to focus on the virtue of humility. Humility is knowing you are **not** better than other people. When Christian leaders and ministries begin to practice true humility, a new platform or template will be created. Imagine what the church would look like when pastors and other leaders view themselves as lower than the rest of the body. No longer comparing one person to another. No longer comparing positions. Not only will the *form* change but the *function* as well.

We all need to be willing to admit that perhaps we have been incorrectly taught. True humility will help us to see that sometimes we have made the Bible say something that it does not really say and have read into the scripture a meaning that was not intended. Our interpretation has not been correct, while our application has drawn conclusions that are inaccurate. I am not suggesting we do away with the basic tenants of the faith. The various doctrines we term as non-essential are often the ones we most misunderstand and the ones that tend to divide us. The adherence to religious tradition can be so strong that it can blind us to the reality of the Gospel of Christ. Like a car, we all have a blind spot and we need help to see. This requires humility. The process to remove the scales from our eyes may be uncomfortable, but so worth it when we see clearly and our understanding is enlightened. Religious traditions are like a hook in a fish. The fish is stuck. The fish needs someone to remove the hook. Once the hook is removed, the fish can be free to swim. Humility, when we own it, will allow someone else to remove the hook. The Gospel of Christ is all about Him, Jesus. Everything points to Him. When we fail to do this, we miss the point altogether.

THE GOAL

We have passed down church traditions without considering that these **traditions** may be the very things that hinder us from being whole as a body. The book of Galatians has a fascinating story of **how** the Apostle Paul came to **know** the Gospel so well.

Galatians 1:1-24, "Paul, an apostle (not of man neither by man, but by Jesus Christ, and God the Father who raised Him from the dead), and all the brethren who are with me, unto the churches of Galatia: Grace be to you and peace from God the Father, and from our Lord Jesus Christ, who gave Himself for our sins, that He might deliver us from this present evil age, according to the will of our God and our Father, to whom be glory forever and ever. Amen.
I marvel that you are so soon removed from Him who called you into the **grace** of Christ, unto another gospel, which is not another; but there be some who trouble you and would pervert the gospel of Christ. But though we, or an angel from heaven, preach any other gospel unto you than what we have preached unto you, let him be accursed. As we have said before, so say I now again, if anyone preaches any other gospel unto you than what you have received, let him be accursed. For do I now persuade men, or God? Or do I seek to please men? For if I yet pleased men, I would not be a servant of Christ. But I certify (make known to) you,

brethren, that the gospel which was preached by me is **not after** (according to) **man**. For I neither received it from man, neither was I taught it, but by (it came through) the **revelation** of Jesus Christ.

For you have heard of my conversation in time past in the Jew's religion, how that beyond measure I persecuted the church of God and wasted it: And profited it the Jew's religion (Judaism) above many my equals in mine own nation, being more exceedingly zealous for the **traditions** of my fathers. But when it pleased God, who separated me from my mother's womb and called me by His grace, *to reveal His Son* in me, that I might preach Him among the heathen (Gentiles); immediately I did not confer with flesh and blood: neither went I up to Jerusalem to those who were apostles before me; but I went into Arabia, and returned again to Damascus.

Then **after three years** I went up to Jerusalem to see Peter, and abode with him fifteen days. But other of the Apostles saw I none, save James the Lord's brother.

Now the things which I write unto you, behold, before God, I lie not. Afterward I came into the regions of Syria and Cilicia; And was unknown by face to the churches of Judea which were in Christ. But they heard only, that he which persecuted us in times past now preacheth the faith which once he destroyed. And they glorified God in me."

We can clearly see that the Christian church is lacking **genuine revelation of Jesus**, His heart, His life, His purpose, His nature, His gifting, His Healing presence, His insight and application of doctrine, His prophetic ability to see into every heart and every need. **We desperately need what the Apostle Paul had, the ability to hear the voice of Jesus**. We need to have God reveal and unveil the scripture to us in a way that is profound and life changing.

I never went to seminary nor went to Bible college, but I did spend many decades in churches learning. I found myself just regurgitating the doctrines I learned. I noticed the same pattern of religious thought in others. It was by much prayer that I began to understand our churches today have a theater atmosphere. The church members tend to be spectators rather than participants.

The main focal point of our modern Christian church service has become the sermon. Instead of gathering together to experience His presence, **we gather together to hear a message** the pastor has diligently studied to prepare. This form was well and good many years ago when society was different, but to continue to use this form in the age of technology is simply no longer needed.

THE FORM

The institutional church has become proficient with technology as to sound systems, instrumentation, styles of music and contemporary worship, video and visual presentations, use of digital media and social media. Despite the use of technology we seem stuck in the format known as the order of service. It has become highly predictable.

The order is as follows:

1. Greeting
2. Songs of worship
3. Announcements
4. Tithes and other offerings
5. The Pastor's message
6. Closing song

This kind of structure does have some value in that it creates a sense of security for those who are sensitive to change. The result has been to create over time a culture of cookie-cutter churches. The average Christian has come to expect that to be all there is. By default many have become complacent to be just another cog in a religious machine. The image presented is that we are building His church. I suggest that when the majority of church attendees are spectators rather than participants, we are not truly building the body. I have heard many sermons on this very subject as to asking people not to be just spectators, yet ironically it is the very **form** we use that prevents full participation and growth in the body. There is a temptation to see people as projects, but people have value simply because they are a creation of God. I suggest seeing the church service as a training place for people to launch from, not to. The purpose of church meetings should be to inspire people to be an influence on culture.

I suggest replacing the current structure with a new church model. This can be tailored for each particular expression of the local body. The first step would be to ensure worship remains worship; to break the mold of a song list and our focus on words and time. A basic outline of a few songs is fine, but the purpose is to help everyone become tuned into the very heart and presence of God, to be intentional on creating a sense of flow with times of just simple chord progressions. Less talk, more focus on feeling the heart of God. The purpose being to enter into His presence.

The message portion should be shorter and concise. The internet has changed everything except our length of sermons. We could start to present the message in a very condensed way, 20 minutes tops. Then present four highly recommended sources that individual members can look up online during the week for further growth. This can be websites, blogs, and social media. Longer messages can occur within the context of seminars.

We must realize that the internet has changed our accessibility to Biblical teaching. A student of the Bible can peruse thousands of sermons and topical teachings at any time they desire. In fact the average person attending church can go online while sitting in church and gather more information about the topic presented than the pastor could possibly even speak about, and do so faster than the pastor could even present it. Pastors and other church leaders need to adapt to an entirely new cultural shift. They should transition from an information-based sermon to a cultural context presentation. That is, to present the message in a way that is relevant to this internet-crazed culture and help them contextualize it so it becomes useful.

The next portion of the service should be a time of prayer. This may take on various forms, such as the church deciding to form a prayer team from their congregation. The team would be comprised of ordinary people who have a compassion for others and not necessarily someone who has a position in the church.

The team would have some basic training and wouldn't have to go through a bureaucracy of classes and certification. Keep it simple. Once a team is ready then anyone who needs prayer can come forward for personal prayer. A rather casual way for the body to pray for one another is to have one row of seats turn around and pray for the opposite row, or have people breaking into groups of ten.

The goal is to be open and creative and not have focus on policy or procedure. Instead, the focus should be more on **function,** that is each member being able to sense the flow of the love and compassion of Jesus extended to others for the needs presented.

A church may desire to have some basic ground rules such as being respectful, gentle and patient. There will most likely be a time of transition and learning as they grow into this experience. This model of a local church expression tends to be more **body focused** than pastor focused. The pastor and other church leaders would need to transition from a positional platform to a servant facilitator **function**. Quite a transition, I know. This begins to make sense when we look at the function of the **body of Christ** as Paul and Peter described.

THE FUNCTION

Ephesians 4:16, Jesus Christ is the head of the church, "from whom the whole body, being fitted and held together by what **every** joint supplies, according to the **proper working** of each individual part, causes the growth of the body for the building up of itself in love."(NASB)

Take time to consider that for the body to be whole and mature, each individual part needs to be whole and mature. This takes time and energy. Life is activated where connection exists.

Ephesians 4:12-13, "His intention was the perfecting and the full equipping of the saints (Body) {that **they** should do} the work of ministering toward the building up of the church. {That it might develop} until we all attain oneness in the faith and in the comprehension of the {full and accurate} knowledge of the Son of God, that {we might arrive} at really mature manhood, the measure of the stature of the fullness of Christ and the completeness found in Him."(Amp)

This translation unpacks the concept that **body ministry is designed by God** for the purpose of becoming healthy and mature as a body.

1 Peter 4:10-11, "As each of **you** has received a gift (a particular **spiritual** talent, a gracious divine endowment) employ it for one another as good trustees of God's many sided grace {faithful stewards of the extremely diverse powers and gifts granted to Christians by unmerited favor}. Whoever speaks {Let him do it as one who utters} oracles of God; whoever renders service as with the strength which God furnishes abundantly, so that in all things God may be glorified through Jesus Christ." (Amp)

Here again we see an emphasis on body ministry. Notice the pastor is not the only one qualified to speak. Both Peter and Paul encourage the use of spiritual gifts as well as natural talents.

We tend to plug people into various positions in the local church based on personalities and surveys. This formula is acceptable for day to day operations, yet there seems to be a lack in allowing spiritual gifting to flow **from within** the body.

The ability to have each member discover the nature and function of their particular part cannot be fully matured by mere programs alone. The way each member functions to the fullest comes by relational integration. The way this looks is to model a healthy family. The family needs structure, however, each member also needs levels of responsibilities and independence without being micromanaged. Leaders in the church would be wise to build small and slow rather than big and fast. Leaders need to do a better job at creating a culture of interdependence, that is each member being mutually dependent on each other rather than dependent on a pastor.

Chapter 2

A Disabled Body

The roles we tend to deem vital in the local church are largely reserved for the pastor and other church leaders. We have clearly seen from scripture that this is merely a part of what the church needs to be fully mature. When we see someone who does not have full function of their body we view them as disabled. A disabled person has a condition that limits movement, senses or activities. In many cases, the brain has perfect normal ability to function, however due to some impairment the rest of the body cannot carry out the desires of the brain, and thus the **body** is not able to function as it should. Jesus is the head of the church and we collectively are His body.(Colossians 1:18).

We have seen in chapter one that it is the body itself where ministry is designed to happen. The institutionalized church has structure, order, policies, procedures and programs. All these are good and have value. In fact, 1 Corinthians 14:40 says, "Let all things be done decently and in order." The context of this verse was the Apostle Paul dealing with various questions and conduct regarding the use of spiritual gifts. We can find a very useful principle here that may be applied to all church life and function: that all things must be done decently and in order. The implication is for conduct to be without chaos. Notice as well the other items that are often overlooked. **The word Let. The word all. The word things.** Paul said so much with so few words here that it is worth great ponderance.

Take a look at a typical church service. How many things are allowed to happen? How many things are not allowed to happen? Make a list. Compare the list to the word *all*. Now consider our comparison to the human body. What would happen if I placed limits on various parts of the body? What if I told the hand it was not allowed to use a spoon or a fork. This may sound silly but the point is too many rules, too many restrictions and suddenly the body becomes disabled. This is when our order cripples our function.

1 Corinthians 14:26, "What then is the right course, believers? When you meet together, **each one** has a psalm, **a teaching**, a revelation, a tongue, or an interpretation. Let everything be constructive and edifying and done for the good of all the church." (Amp)

A detailed description of "Let all things" is provided in chapter five under the subtitle of, How do we get from where we are to where they were?

Chapter 3

To Tithe Or Not To Tithe

To tithe or not to tithe is obviously a reference to the opening phrase from Hamlet, a famous play by Shakespeare. The words from Hamlet are, "To be or not to be." I chose this play on words so we can have a phrase to ponder while taking a thorough look at the subject of tithing.

A tithe simply means a tenth or ten percent. It is very common among religious organizations to ask people who are members involved in that particular organization to tithe. That is, they ask members to give ten percent of their income to their group. The practice of tithing has been around for thousands of years. The people of Israel were instructed to do so as found in the book of Numbers, Deuteronomy and Malachi. Jesus made a reference to this practice as well (Matthew 23:23). The doctrine of the tithe continues today in most Christian churches.

The question some people ask is: Why do most churches expect members to tithe? Is it a requirement? There are many religious rules and rituals which were observed thousands of years ago that we no longer follow. For example, we no longer sacrifice animals at the altar. We no longer have slaves, yet the Bible refers to slaves. In fact, even in the New Testament it says, "Masters treat your slaves justly and fairly, because you know that you also have a master in heaven." (Colossians 4:1) Does this imply that it is okay for a Christian to own a slave? I think not.

I recall a book written many years ago about a Jewish man who came to realize Jesus was his Messiah, the Jewish Messiah. The book was called, "They Thought For Themselves." I encourage you to do the same as we take a fresh look at this subject. Take time and thought to consider context, purpose, intention and application of the various verses from the Bible that mention the tithe. Consider what Jesus taught concerning it.

Consider as well what the apostles taught and how often they taught it. Compare the results you find with what is taught in the church today. A 2008 article in *Christianity Today* provides a very good summary of the history of the tithe.

"Most discussions of tithing begin with the Old Testament precedent, first recorded in Genesis 14:20. After winning an astounding victory in battle and retrieving his nephew Lot along with all his lost possessions, Abram thanked God by giving Melchizedek one-tenth of all he had. Then, in Numbers 18:21, we find tithing included in the Mosaic Law. Its purpose was to provide for the Levites, whom God wanted to concentrate on priestly duties. While the New Testament contains no explicit command to tithe, many have argued that this relationship between the Levites and the other tribes of Israel prefigures how Christians should provide for their ministers. This view

of tithing, known as parallelism, gained prominence in the church around the sixth century.

Many non-Jewish and pre-Christian societies also practiced tithing-like giving. Some ancient sources describe how kings imposed a type of first-fruits tax to maintain holy shrines and support clergy. From Nebuchadnezzar's Babylonia to the temples of Apollo in Delphi and Athena in Athens, pre-Christian centers of worship collected tithes for their gods. Ancient cultures as disparate as the Greeks and Chinese—including the Arabians, Phoenicians, Romans, and Carthaginians—gave in ways mirroring the tithe. Some scholars believe ancient cultures hit on the seemingly arbitrary figure of one-tenth because they often did calculations on their fingers.

The early church's views on tithing foreshadowed many of today's stewardship debates. The Eastern Church began tithing out of obligation because they believed Jesus' conversation with the rich young man demanded sacrificial generosity. Clement of Alexandria and Irenaeus pleaded with the church to surpass even the Old Testament tithe since Christ had freed them from the Law. Later church fathers—John Chrysostom, Cyprian, Origen, and Augustine among them—complained from time to time that their followers lacked Christian charity. Chrysostom even shamed his stingy church for marveling at those who tithed. He contrasted their amazement with the dutiful giving of Old Testament Jews.

The early church's expectation that every Christian would tithe found formal expression at the Synod of

Mâçon in 585, which embedded the practice in canon law. A millennium later, the Council of Trent sharpened this law's teeth: it provided for excommunication if any Catholic declined to contribute his tithe. This, despite the stain in the Church's monetary record that Luther had so recently uncovered in his critique of papal indulgences.

Post-Reformation Europe, however, didn't do much better: in the centuries after Luther, secular governments often acted on behalf of the churches by collecting mandatory tithes. These more closely resembled American property taxes than Jewish monetary offerings. Without a state-imposed tithe, giving in the United States developed quite differently than in Europe. American church leaders have often emphasized the New Testament's command to give freely and cheerfully, which some leaders have cited to advocate giving less or even more than ten percent. As a result, tithing has been practiced only sporadically in the modern church..."

It seems that many people who are in ministry expect all Christians to tithe. There seems to be an entitlement mentality for some who are in ministry. Why? Perhaps one reason may come from reading **into** portions of the Bible such as:

Numbers 18:21, "And behold, I have given the children of Levi all the tenth in Israel for an inheritance, for their service which they serve, even the service of the tabernacle of the congregation."

Many pastors and other ministries apply this verse to themselves by suggesting that a pastor is a New Testament version of the Levitical priesthood. They suggest a pastor provides service for each congregation and as such are entitled to be paid from the tithes of the church. I can see how this may feel like an appropriate application of this verse, yet when we consider the whole subject matter this application falls apart.

The reason the priest was to partake of part of the funds from the tithe is that under the Mosaic law they were **not allowed** to own anything nor earn a living. They were the Levitical priesthood. A priesthood we will later see was done away with as Jesus died, and upon His death a New Testament became enforced. A New Covenant with better promises. (Hebrews 8:6)

Take time to really think that through. Can a pastor or any minister find a job and own property of any kind? In our society are they allowed? We need to rethink how we apply the scripture. We should have due diligence in proper application and not attempt to make the Bible say something that it does not say in order to fit our doctrinal stance.

Imagine Jesus talking about cars, airplanes, cell phones and computers. That may seem like a ridiculous idea, but I present this in order to provoke a thought process called **frame of reference.** For example, in the day Jesus lived when someone talked about light, what would they be referring to? Fire of some kind, of course. They would not be thinking of electricity and light bulbs. They would think of lamps filled with oil and a lit wick. A torch perhaps as well. That is frame of reference. This is a valuable tool when reading and understanding the Bible.

We can now look at the people who were first instructed to tithe, the Hebrews who lived thousands of years ago. Instead of seeing the tithe within the frame of reference of modern society and governments, take the time to consider that the Hebrews were a nation unto themselves. In essence God, the prophets and the Levites who acted as priests *were* the government. Now take a fresh step back in time and discover the main purpose and intention of an instruction to tithe.

Deuteronomy 14:22-28, "You shall surely tithe all the produce from what you sow, which comes out of the field every year. You shall eat in the presence of the Lord your God, at the place where He chooses to establish His name, the tithe of your grain, your new wine, your oil, and the firstborn of your herd and of your flock; so that you may learn to fear the Lord your God always. If the distance is so great for you, that you are not able to carry it (the tithe), since the place where the Lord your God chooses to set His name is too far away from you when the Lord your God blesses you, then you shall exchange it for money, and bind the money in your hand and go to the place which the Lord your God chooses. You may spend the money for **whatever your heart desires**: for oxen, or sheep, or wine, or strong drink, or for whatever your heart desires; and **there you shall eat** in the presence the Lord your God **and rejoice, you and your household**. Also you shall not neglect the Levite who is in your town, **for he has no portion or inheritance among you**. At the end of every third year you shall bring out all the tithe of your produce in that year, and shall deposit it in your town. The Levite because he has no portion or inheritance among you, and the stranger, the orphan, and the widow, who are in your town, **shall come, and eat and be satisfied**, in order that the Lord your God may bless you in all the work of your hand which you do."(NASB)

We need to note the original **purpose and use of the tithe**. The context seems to indicate this was as much **about a celebration** as anything else. Notice a family was to tithe year by year according to the yield of the harvest. They also were required to bring the first born of the herds and sheep that year. It would seem this is a part of the Mosaic law. Deuteronomy is the fifth book in the Torah and was written by Moses (Deuteronomy 1:1). The book itself means second law and offers a restatement of the law for a new generation.

The Jewish nation, even in the time of Jesus, followed these rules. Notice further that if a family could not travel, they could sell the food and animals for money and then spend that money on anything they desired! Imagine a church today telling the members to save up ten percent of their income and then at the end of the year take that money and spend it on themselves and have a big celebration! Could it be that God actually loves people and wants them to enjoy the work of their hands by taking time to celebrate all the hard work? Then of course those who could travel and bring the tithe to the storehouse would also participate in a feast of celebration, as would the Levites, and the widow, and the fatherless, and the stranger. The excess food and livestock would be stored up to support the Levitical priesthood for the year as well as provide for the widow and the fatherless.

Furthermore, does this program not also look similar to our modern social programs in providing basic needs for those who cannot provide it themselves? Has anyone ever heard a politician propose a flat tax of ten percent? Again remember the Hebrews were a nation unto themselves. They were a theocratic nation.

Could the instruction to tithe be as simple and as practical as a structured social system to make sure everyone was provided for and no one left in dire need? Could it be that God cares for people in this manner? Could it be this simple?

This may be a new concept for many Christians. I hope you are beginning to see things you never saw before. I hope that your understanding becomes enlightened by the Holy Spirit and you have fresh revelation so you live not by the letter of the law but by the life it was intended to produce.

Malachi Chapter Three is the most widely used chapter from the Bible concerning the tithe. I spent years quoting this chapter as part of my regimen before I sought out the context and purpose. I gained even greater contextual understanding when I weighed these Old Testament (covenant) chapters against the New Testament (covenant) verses and found an amazing lack of instruction to the newly formed body of believers concerning the tithe. It would be time well spent to read the entire book of Malachi in order to attain a better perspective. Malachi was written hundreds of years after Deuteronomy. This is important to note because when we truly understand the purpose of the tithe, we can clearly see that **all Malachi did was to point out the Mosaic rules which the Jews were neglecting. Should we be placed under mosaic rules too?**

    The prophet speaking on behalf of God brings correction to the priests in Chapter One. They were the church leaders of that time. They offered defiled animal sacrifices when they knew better. The basic message here is the leaders said one thing with their mouth but did the exact opposite in their actions. The contextual correction being spoken here is to address the hypocrisy of the leaders, those who represent God.

    Malachi Chapter Two continues with this issue and God tells the priests (leaders) He will not hear them and furthermore they are cursed because of their <u>**hardness of heart**</u>. I cannot recall ever hearing this context presented when listening to a sermon about the tithe. When we take the time and effort to read the passages that are often overlooked, we begin to see what we never saw before.

Break From The System

When we follow tradition and overlook culture, context, purpose and intention, it becomes easy for us to make the Bible say something that it is not saying and apply the meaning to a people it is not applicable to. Why do we do that? We simply do not ask the penetrating questions that help us think for ourselves.

Malachi 3:8-12, "Will a man rob God? In what way have we robbed God? In tithes and offerings. You are cursed...for you have robbed me. **Even this whole nation**. Bring all the tithes into the **storehouse** in order that **there may be food in my house**. And try me now in this, if I will not open the windows of heaven and pour out for you such a blessing that there will **not be room enough to receive it**. And I will rebuke the devourer for your sake so that he will not destroy the fruit of your ground, nor will the vine fail to bear fruit for you in the field. And **all nations shall call you blessed**. For you will be a delightful land." (NKJV)

The purpose of the tithe stated here is to provide an abundance of **food**. When we connect this to the Mosaic law as found in Numbers and Deuteronomy, it is clear this is talking about an agricultural society who stored the grain in large holding units. This is frame of reference, the Mosaic law and food. I can also picture the classic movie, "The Ten Commandments" and the scene where Moses opens the silos where the grain is stored so the slaves could gather food. This is the storehouse. It was set aside for a specific people, the Levites and also to be distributed to the poor.

A pastor may often claim that the local church is the new testament version of the storehouse. In other words, a pastor who feeds the people spiritual food by teaching the Bible and providing other services such as counseling and administration is to be provided for with the tithes. This parallelism is quite a stretch! We no longer have a centralized temple where sacrifices are offered for the remission of sin! We, the body of Christ, all of us and each of us are the very temple of God. We also no longer have a Levitical priesthood. We are all now a royal priesthood (1Peter 2:9) because of Jesus. Also, as stated before, a pastor today is allowed to participate in society and enjoy all the benefits thereof.

So go back and read those verses again keeping in mind this frame of reference. Does it take on a new meaning? A new revelation? When we use Malachi Chapter Three to inspire people to tithe, we are actually telling people they need to keep the Mosaic laws. Some people have referred to a statement Jesus made to the Pharisees (Matthew 23:23) as a validation to tithe. Well, of course Jesus would tell Jews who still observed the Mosaic laws that they should not neglect to follow those laws.

The Jewish temple still existed. They still sacrificed animals when Jesus walked the earth. He did not tell them to stop the sacrifices. Think about it! The very day Jesus died as a sacrifice for our sins, the high priest was sacrificing a lamb. Furthermore, Jesus spoke to thousands of people at a time. It is simply not recorded anywhere that he told people to tithe. Why did Jesus not act like modern pastors in this regard?

There are some pastors who will quote from 1 Corinthians Chapter Nine as grounds for a pastor to be paid a salary. A thorough look at that chapter will reveal Paul was not talking about pastors but rather apostolic ministry. Paul uses phrases such as; "Am I not an apostle, Are you not my work in the Lord." Also, he mentions the seal of his apostleship. Paul further asks, "who plants a vineyard and does not eat of the fruit or who tends a flock and does not drink some of the milk?" Paul later conveys the idea that those who preach the gospel should live from the gospel. Yet Paul says he used none of these rights and further that he has written this in order that no such provision be made for him. The position Paul presents hardly represents the compensation package most pastors of today are allotted.

What Does The New Testament Say About Tithing?

The Bible is divided into two sections. The Old Testament and the New Testament. It is true that **all** scripture is inspired and profitable for instruction (2 Timothy 3:16). It is also true that when Jesus died the New Testament came into effect.

"For where a testament is, there must also be the death of the testator." (Hebrews 9:16)

This holds true for anyone who is wise enough to have a legal last will and testament. We live in New Testament times. We need to be fully aware of New Testament terms and realities so we can best apply the benefits. Again, all scripture is inspired yet my point is simply this, **Jesus changed everything!** What does the New Testament say about tithing? Actually very little! Surprised?

Matthew 23:23, Jesus was talking to the Pharisees. Jesus said to them, "Woe unto you, scribes and Pharisees, hypocrites! for ye pay **tithe** of mint and anise and cummin (herbs) and have omitted the weightier matters **of the law**, judgment, mercy, and faith; these ought ye to have done, and not to leave the other undone." Notice Jesus refers to the tithe as part of the law.

Hebrews Chapter Seven retells the story of Abraham who tithed of the spoils of war. There are other places in the New Testament where money or free will offerings are spoken of. But for now consider here the frame of reference and contextual understanding; the New Testament mentions tithing in the context of the Old Testament. Jesus talked about the Pharisees who lived strictly under the Old Testament laws and other traditions and restrictions. Jesus did indicate that the Pharisees should not neglect the tithe. The question few ask is, "**did Jesus tell the common people to tithe?**" **If not, why not?**

After Jesus resurrected, He also appeared to the disciples and the church was born and began to grow. We can see then how the early church talked about giving and what instructions concerning money the apostles and other church leaders disseminated. A fine example would be 2 Corinthians 9:7, "So let each one give as he **purposes** in his heart, not grudgingly or of **necessity**; for God loves a cheerful giver." (NKJV).

The word *purposes* according to the concordance means to "***choose for one's self.***" Take time to really think that through. Paul is telling the Christians at the church of Corinth to give whatever amount **they choose to**. Imagine in this context if someone decided to give two percent. Would this be acceptable? Yes! The word *necessity* means to do by constraint, or compulsion. We all can picture the typical church service and the offering time. Compare and contrast that with these instructions by Paul.

A very similar instruction on giving can be seen in 2 Corinthians 8:12, "For if there is a willing mind, it is accepted according to what one has, and not according to what one does not have." (NKJV)

The amplified version translates it this way, "For if the eagerness to give is there, then it is accepted and welcome **in proportion to what a person has**, and not what one does not have." Think about the implications. There seems to be a great amount of Grace being extended here by Paul. Not everyone is expected to give unless there is a willing and eager desire to give. The **amount** is determined not only by what **each person chooses** for themselves but also in proportion to what **they can actually afford**. Allow this thought to sink in. **This needs to be the mainstream teaching in the church concerning giving.**

A brief description of the church at Corinth will help us gain contextual understanding. Paul visited Corinth about 52 AD. Paul became acquainted with Priscilla and Aquila who were tent makers. Most likely this is what Paul used to initiate a conversation and relationship as Paul himself was a tent maker by trade. He preached about Jesus. The body of believers there began to grow. The church in Corinth consisted principally of non-Jews (1 Corinthians 12:2). Paul had no intention at first of making the city a base of operations (Acts 18:1; Acts 16:9, 10). His plans were changed by a revelation (Acts 18:9, 10). The Lord commanded him to speak boldly, and he did so, remaining in the city eighteen months.

Finding strong opposition in the synagogue he left the Jews and went to the Gentiles (Acts 18:6). Nevertheless, Crispus, the ruler of the synagogue and his household were believers and baptisms were numerous (Acts 18:8). One of these, Gaius, was Paul's host the next time he visited the city (Romans 16:23). Silas and Timothy, who had been left at Berea, came to Corinth about forty-five days after Paul's arrival.

Within a few years after Paul's first visit to Corinth the Christians had increased so rapidly that they made quite a large congregation, but it was composed mainly of the lower classes: they were neither learned, influential, nor of noble birth (1 Corinthians 1:26).

Paul started many of these early churches so it is worth the time to examine how Paul conducted himself as a leader and how he viewed giving. We saw what Paul taught concerning giving. He never mentioned a tithe. He taught giving in proportion to what each person can afford. He also taught by example.

Look at Acts 18:1-3, "After these things Paul departed from Athens and **went to Corinth**. And he found a certain Jew named Aquilla who had recently come from Italy with his wife Priscilla...so because he (Paul) was of the same trade, he stayed with them and **worked**; for by occupation they were tent makers."

Acts 18:11 says Paul stayed there eighteen months. It is within all reason to believe **Paul worked** during that time to support himself. As stated the church at Corinth was comprised largely of non-Jews (Gentiles). People who were mostly uneducated and strangers from the traditions and covenants of the Jews. Those who may not have known about the custom of the tithe and who most certainly never practiced it. So why did Paul fail to teach them to tithe? Is it not obvious that Paul believed it was no longer required?

Acts Chapter Fifteen talks about a question concerning the Gentiles in other cities who became Christians. The question was concerning circumcision, yet we can learn much here. Paul and Barnabas went to see the other apostles and elders to hear about this dispute. This is what they concluded.

Acts 15:28-29, "For it has seemed right to the Holy Spirit and to us to lay **no further burden upon you** except what is absolutely essential, namely, that you avoid what has been sacrificed to idols, tasting blood, eating the meat of whatever has been strangled and sexual immorality. Keep yourselves clear of these things and you will make good progress. Farewell."(J B Phillips)

Why did this company of great men not mention the tithe to the early gentile believers? Have you ever stopped long enough to ask that question? Think about the implications. If you were a Jewish believer in Jesus back then and had the incredible experience of birthing hundreds of new churches filled with thousands of Jews and Gentiles, would the tithe not also be in your written letter of instructions? Would it not also be a necessary basic teaching?

The apostles did teach people to love one another, practice hospitality and to be generous. They taught about sowing and reaping as did Jesus. Yet, it seems clear that they did not teach an obligation to tithe. They also did not expect the churches to pay them salaries. They did not present themselves with a sense of entitlement. They did humbly accept food and lodging and some supplies, but the pervasive attitude was one of working with one's own hands in order **to set an example** of conduct.

2 Thessalonians 3:6-9, "But we command ye, brethren, in the name of our Lord Jesus Christ, that you withdraw from every brother who walks disorderly and not according to the tradition which he received from us. For ye yourselves know how ye ought to follow **us**, for **we behaved ourselves not** disorderly among you; **nor did we eat** anyone's bread **free of charge**, but wrought with labor and travail night and day, that we might not be chargeable to any of you: not that we do not have authority, **but to make ourselves an example of how you should follow us.**"

The first thing to note here is that Paul was not just talking about himself. He used terms such as **us and we**. He most likely was referring to Silas and Timothy as well as others. The context defines disorderly as someone who will not work. This would by default in context include church leaders. These apostles and church leaders worked so as to set an example of conduct. So is this example for the body only? Could it not also be an example for those in ministry? We need to ask these thought-provoking questions in order to truly find a correct application. We need to discover the heart of Jesus and ministry. The apostles did not eat without paying for it. They worked with labor and hardship. Reminds me of the phrase *"hard work and long nights."* The purpose was to not be a financial burden on the church body for support. They provided their own financial support to offer themselves as a model to be copied.

2 Corinthians 11:7, "Did I do wrong and cheapen myself and make you look down on me because I preached God's Good News to you without charging you anything? "(TLB).

So here we have again Paul writing to the church at Corinth about his service to them. His **free** service. To be fair Paul did receive offerings from other churches as stated in the next verse, but we would be wise to get a clear picture as to the heart of ministry as presented by Paul: **Make it free whenever possible**.

2 Corinthians 11:8-9, "I took wages from other churches in order to minister to you. And when I was present with you, and in need, I was a burden to no one, for what I lacked the brethren who came from Macedonia supplied. So I kept myself from being a burden to you in any way, **and will continue to do so**."(NKJV)

The amplified version defines the brothers as Silas and Timothy and the supplies coming from the church at Philipi. Some would be tempted to focus on the latter verses where Paul and Timothy actually accepted wages, however consider the full context. Paul relates the story in Philippians.

"I know how to be abased and I know how to abound. Everywhere and in all things I have learned both to be full and **to be hungry**, both to be full and

to suffer need. I can do all things through Christ who strengthens me. Nevertheless you have done well that you shared in my **distress**." (Philippians 4:12-14)

The full story can be illustrated by considering all the pieces of the puzzle. It seems that despite the hard work Paul did, there were many times he was short on money, food and supplies.

Paul was so determined to supply ministry free of charge that **he chose** to suffer need and hunger rather than ask the church to give him aid. That would include times of fasting. That would include the inability to purchase raw materials in order to make the tents he would sell. A small business disaster! The time frame of these episodes of distress is not clear. I am sure travel to and from these cities while carrying supplies would be time consuming and even somewhat dangerous due to hardships and even possibly being robbed. Paul may have waited weeks, even months for new supplies. He would therefore be forced to ration out wisely what he did have. This is what Paul meant when he wrote, "I can do all things through Christ who strengthens me." We quote this so glibly without having the understanding of the circumstances.

Now that we have a better and more excellent understanding of how Paul, Timothy, Silas, and the other apostles related the use of money and the purposes of ministry and giving, we must admit this is a drastic paradigm shift compared to the accepted teaching in most churches. If we desire to copy these great men and founders of the Christian Church, it requires **a total paradigm shift as to how we do what we do.**

We need to see that believers today are not part of a theocratic nation, as was Israel. We are not obligated to tithe. We will not face negative consequences if we do not tithe. God will not be mad at us. God will not withhold blessings. Conversely, God is not obligated to bless us if we do tithe. This may be an entire new way of thinking for some. It simply depends on what type of lens we see through. It is often said God sees us through the sacrifice of Jesus. We accept this in regards to sin. We accept this in regards to righteousness and works. Why not the tithe? Some church leaders act as if the tithe has more power than the sacrifice Jesus made with His own innocent blood!

What About Abraham And The Tithe?

There are some who believe that as Christians we are not obligated to tithe as concerning the law. The very same people also contend that Abraham tithed before the law came and as such we should follow this as an example of a tithe of faith.

Hebrews 7:1-10, "For this Melchizedek, king of Salem, priest of the most high God, who met Abraham returning from the slaughter of the kings and blessed him (Abraham), to whom also Abraham gave a tenth part of all, first being translated king of righteousness and then also king of Salem, meaning king of peace, without father, without mother, without genealogy, having neither beginning of days nor end of life, but **made like the Son of God**, remains a priest continually.

Now consider how great this man was, to whom even the great patriarch **Abraham gave a tenth of the spoils**. And indeed those who are of the sons of Levi, who receive the priesthood, have a commandment to receive tithes from the people according to the law, that is from their brethren, though they have come from the loins of Abraham; but he whose genealogy is not derived from them received tithes from Abraham and blessed him who had the promises. Now beyond all contradiction the lesser is blessed by the better.

Here mortal men receive tithes, **but there** he receives them, of whom it is witnessed that he lives. **Even Levi** who receives tithes, **paid tithes through Abraham so to speak** for he was still in the loins of his father (Abraham) when Melchizedek met him." (NKJV)

Let us consider, without speculation, what can clearly be seen in the story. This tithe appears to be completely voluntary on the part of Abraham. There is not any indication that God had instructed Abraham to do this. The **tithe was given from the spoils of war**. That means **Abraham did not use his own money to tithe from**. Think about the implications when we teach the tithe of Abraham.

We also must remember to use frame of reference whenever possible. Thousands of years ago kings would often war with each other. The victor would often plunder the goods of the city they conquered. They might even take over the control of the city and set up a governor. Imagine how bizarre it would be today if one church conquered another church and just took all the possessions. Honestly, who would do that? The word spoils here means top of the heap. We can picture this like a scene from a movie. Items piled high in a heap. Abraham probably had his men take the top of the pile and hand it over to Melchizedek. If we want to make a parallel application of the tithe of Abraham, we would need to find a Christian who has so many possessions that they are literally piled up and way more than one would need for living.

Abraham tithed to this Melchizedek who had no genealogy. No father. No mother. No beginning. No end. Who is like the Son of God. A priest forever. Who does this description fit best? This is obviously a type and shadow of Jesus, which is a very common theme throughout the Bible. The story of Shadrach, Meshach and Abednego, as found in the book of Daniel 3:19-27, is a very good example of this type and shadow of Jesus. These three men would not bow down to the idols of the King and so the King ordered these three men to be placed in a furnace. More like a giant pit of fire in those days. A miracle happened: the men were not burned. Why? There was a fourth man seen in the furnace. One who looked like the Son of God. This happened long before Jesus was born. How? He is the Alpha and Omega. The beginning and the end.

Abraham did not tithe to a human. On Earth, men receive tithes under the law (rules). In Heaven, He receives tithes. So we can see the physical and spiritual being represented. The reason we fail to understand mysteries is we focus on the physical, earthly substance. That is all we can see. Many people expected Jesus to set up an earthly kingdom and thus missed the substance of the spiritual kingdom. The mystery of the tithe is; Jesus fulfilled it to the utmost by His death and resurrection and actually abolished it by His blood sacrifice. It says Levi already tithed because he was in the seed of Abraham. We, in a sense, have already tithed because we are in Christ and by faith are the seed of Abraham (Galatians 3:29). Furthermore, the **subject** of the narrative is Jesus, not the tithe.

Colossians 2:15, "And (Jesus) having **spoiled** principalities and powers, He made a show of them openly, triumphing over them in it."

It was well known that when one king conquered another, the victor would parade the king who lost before all the people and thus make a public display of the complete victory. Abraham gave a tithe of the spoil. Jesus took the spoil and presented the complete victory to Heaven. Abraham was the material shadow; Jesus was the spiritual substance. The mystery we need to understand can be found in the answer to a question. If I met you on a sunny day would you want me to talk to your shadow or you? Imagine being married and only relating to someone based on their shadow. To understand the tithe of Abraham, all we need is to understand what Jesus did in the spiritual realities of the cross. We know that Jesus did not just take our sin, **He became our sin** (2 Corinthians 5:21). Jesus became the sacrificial lamb (John 1:29).

Jesus became our sabbath (Matthew 11:28). **He** will give us rest, not just a day which was a shadow of things to come. Well for those who are willing to see it, Jesus became the tithe. Romans 8:29, Jesus is the first born among many. In other words **Jesus became the first fruits (tithe)**. Jesus died on Passover and resurrected at the feast of first fruits. It is accepted that Jesus became the Passover Lamb, so why not believe Jesus fulfilled the first fruits? Imagine the audacity of mere humans to think we can possibly undo something Jesus has already done.

Abraham did many physical acts that were prophetic. They pointed to something in the future. They pointed to the spiritual and to Jesus. Abraham presenting his son as a sacrifice for example (Genesis 22). God would send His son Jesus as a sacrifice thousands of years later.

It would be insanity for us today to think we should follow the faith of Abraham in this example. Yet, it is commonly taught to follow the faith of Abraham in the tithe. We thus fail to catch the spiritual significance of these prophetic acts. We have replaced the superior spiritual realm with the inferior natural realm.

The Bottom Line

Now that we have looked at the tithe from various angles, let us consider the practical aspects of the use of money. This is often referred to as stewardship. We all know generosity is a good thing. It truly is a blessed event when we give to others. Our time, our energy, our talents and our money. People from various cultures and beliefs have found this to be true. Christians should be examples of this generous spirit.

The tithe is no longer a requirement. The evidence is overwhelming. **No one should be expected to tithe**. That is not to say that someone cannot tithe if they should so choose. There should be a sense of financial responsibility applied in such cases. Being financially responsible means not having debt, paying all the bills on time, not living above the current means, yet working to provide for oneself and a family if there is one. That means living in a safe and healthy place, having safe transportation, healthy food and decent clothes as well as health care. Once all those items are in place it would be within reason to begin a tithe as a practice if that is what is in the heart to do. To tithe out of an excess supply (spoils) rather than a shortage is indeed a different paradigm.

In the United States the average working American pays about twenty percent in Federal taxes. That money is withheld from the worker. The money withheld (a double tithe) is designed to support infrastructure and social programs. What most people fail to realize is that in a very real and practical way **the Christian who works and pays Federal Income tax is in fact tithing**. Then the institutional church will tell them to tithe to the church. That would be equal to now thirty percent of someone's income. Let us not forget State income tax. That could be another ten percent. Add in sales tax, health care expense and dozens of other hidden fees and taxes, and the average person is financially burdened. Jesus would not desire to increase burdens, but rather *His* burden is light (Matthew 11:30).

Chapter 4

<u>The Pastors Place</u>

Jeremiah 3:15. "I will give you pastors according to **mine heart**, who will feed you with knowledge and understanding." This is a great place to start. The word pastor in the Hebrew means to tend a flock, a companion, keep company with, feed and be a friend. When you take time to apply this to our current ideas of a pastor, it creates a paradigm shift as to focus. The word heart in the Hebrew refers to the place of feelings, the **inner most organ**, the will combined with feelings.

Besides Jeremiah, the only place the word pastor itself is used is in the book of Ephesians 4:11, "And He himself gave some to be apostles, some prophets, some evangelists, and some **pastors** and teachers." (NKJV)

The Greek word used here for pastor is *poimon*. It simply means a shepherd. This is worth noting because in both the Old and New Testament a pastor is not portrayed as a king but rather as a servant. It is not a high position. It is not governmental. It is rather common and lowly.

There are many great sources to study the subject of church structures, hence I will not cover those aspects. My goal is to look at perspectives that, although simplistic, are often overlooked. I recently came across the website of a local church that has a structure of a plurality of elders/pastors who are bi-vocational. That means each pastor has a primary secular job and any service they perform for the church is done as unpaid voluntary service. The various pastoral work is shared by all. This is much closer to the intention of the role of a pastor than what we currently see in most churches. The perspectives I present illustrates that the function of a pastor was not intended to be the head of the local church.

What Is A Pastor ?

There are three Greek words used to describe a church leader. Acts Chapter Twenty uses all three terms interchangeably. In verse seventeen, Paul assembles all the **elders** [*presbuteros*] of the church to give them his farewell message.

Acts 20:28, "Be on guard for yourselves and for all the flock, among which the Holy Spirit has made you **overseers** [*episkopos*], to **shepherd or pastor** [*poimon*] the church of God." (NKJV)

These labels are still used in the Episcopal and Presbyterian churches. The terms appear to be interchangeable and seem to be different ways to describe the same thing, although there may be some nuances to each **function**.

First Peter 2:25 says, "For ye were as sheep going astray, but now are returned to the Shepherd [*poimen*] and Bishop [*episkopos or guardian*] of your souls."

Jesus is the great Shepherd/Bishop/Pastor and head of the church body. Jesus is our example. He indeed is a pastor according to **the very heart of God**.

John 1:18, "No man hath seen God at any time, the only begotten Son, which is in the **bosom of the Father**, He hath declared Him."

Rather than follow the traditions of the intellect, it would be better to follow the heart of some simple illustrations.

A shepherd was very commonly used in the Bible for illustrations. We can draw out some hands on lessons from tapping into the heart of the shepherd. The shepherd exists for the sheep. The sheep do not exist for the shepherd. A pastor is there to support the people. The people are not there to support the pastor. This may be a radical thought for many. Think like Jesus would think.

Mark 6:33 notes that Jesus saw people as "sheep without a shepherd." It is for this reason Jesus had compassion on them. To be a pastor means to follow the path of being a shepherd *after the heart* of God.

The Hebrew word for pastor in the passage from Jeremiah carries the meaning of feeding, keeping company with and being a friend. Jesus exemplified all of these qualities. The first miracle that Jesus did was when He was attending a wedding feast. This is found in the Gospel of John 2:1-11. We see Jesus keeping company with others as a good shepherd would naturally do. It is commonly known that this kind of wedding celebration would last for many days, not just a few hours as is common in western culture. This means that Jesus spent significant time with the people there. In other words, Jesus hung out with people. Picture this shepherd of people eating, drinking, dancing, laughing and celebrating life.

"The Son of man (Jesus) has come eating and drinking, and you say behold, a man who is a glutton and a wine drinker, a friend of tax collectors and notorious sinners."(Luke 7:34 Amp)

"One of the Pharisees asked Jesus to dine with him, and He went into the Pharisees house and reclined at table."(Luke 7:36)

What are these verses telling us in todays vernacular? That Jesus hung out with everybody. Jesus was accused of being friends with the worst of the worst. Jesus reclined at table. The custom of enjoying a meal with people lasted for hours and rather than sit in a chair, the custom was to recline. A very intimate setting and time of fellowship.

This is the example of the great shepherd. He loves all types of people. It is true that Jesus was unique in that He would not be corrupted by the behavior of those around him. So, there is wisdom in having boundaries for ourselves. The point is, Jesus could be natural and supernatural at the same time. He was naturally supernatural. He did not isolate himself from the world. He did not see himself as too good or too busy to spend time with people. He influenced others not just by his teaching and not just by his miracles, but also by relational integration. A good shepherd will naturally smell like sheep because he spends so much time in the field next to them.

The last part of the verse from Jeremiah 3:15 mentions a pastor who feeds with knowledge and understanding. This type of pastor is someone who has the ability to draw out and reveal who God is, what He is like, and **impart** the very heart of God. That is what Jesus did. Jesus **declared** the Father and had the ability to **unpack the concept of Father's heart**. This is not intellectualism. This is not mere theology. This is not doctrine. A pastor according to the heart of God teaches others *how to* experience God, how to hear the voice of God, how to display the kingdom of God. A good shepherd teaches others how to live, love, laugh, and be relational. How can one teach what one does not have? How can one teach what one does not live?

Jesus taught as one who had authority. It means He knew what He was talking about and it showed. It was more than head knowledge. It was something that was a part of him, fully integrated and woven into his being so that it simply flowed out from him. **He taught from the heart, not from the head**.

We often miss the simplicity that is in Jesus (2 Corinthians 11:3). Jesus did a few simple things. He did them consistently and He did them very well. Jesus taught the kingdom of God and healed the sick. A good shepherd would always tend to the sick and heal them. Jesus fed, cared for and loved people. Jesus showed great mercy and compassion for people. Jesus cast out demons when needed. Jesus fellowshipped. Jesus demonstrated the spiritual reality of the invisible kingdom of God.

This may sound radical but to follow in the footsteps of Jesus and His example of a pastor after the heart of God, a pastor today should make **all of the above** a part of ministry. We need humility to admit when we do not see this in our life and to realize all of this is needed today. We need humility to receive from God and others the parts we are lacking. Pastors need to rethink what pastoral ministry is.

Some believe all these dramatic events are no longer needed today. Yet, all these dramatic events are an integral part of the Father's heart.

The New Testament reference to a pastor in Ephesians 4:11 mentions pastor in a list with four other ministry functions. The first item we must recognize is that all the ministries mentioned are called **gifts**.

Ephesians 4:7-8, "But unto every one of us is given **grace** according to the measure of the **gift** of Christ. Wherefore He saith, when He ascended up on high, He led captivity captive, and **gave gifts** unto men (anthropos-human being)." Verse 11 picks up the thought and continues with **He** (Jesus) **gave** some apostles, some prophets, some evangelists, and some pastors and teachers."

The Greek word for gave and gifts simply meant a present, a grant, or **something bestowed**. We can correlate this with the free gift of salvation. John 3:16, "For God so loved the world that He **gave** his unique son..." The word *gave* here means the same, to *bestow*. The obvious conclusion is just like salvation, ministry cannot be earned. Salvation and ministry are both a grace gift thus there is a very real and genuine *gift of pastor* to receive.

This list of ministry gifts are often referred to as the fivefold ministry. The list is often illustrated by looking at your hand. The thumb would represent the apostle. The index finger would represent the prophet (used to point the way). The middle finger would represent the evangelist (it reaches furthest as the norm). The ring finger would represent the pastor. The pinky finger would represent the teacher. There are many sources that talk about these ministries as to origins and structure. The purpose of this book is to look at the often overlooked and practical aspects of ministry.

The normal path into these ministries is to attend a Bible college, become certified and ordained, then sent out to be plugged into the network of churches. This system has become the *requirement* to be accepted as an approved minister. This system does have benefits and a measure of safety. Yet, it breeds a general attitude of entitlement and a religious hierarchy. The primary qualification for ministry has become the amount of theology and doctrinal knowledge someone has acquired.

Bible college has a place, but consider what Bible college the early church leaders attended. Today the pastor is the main focus. What role did the pastor have as the early church grew? Why is the pastor the head of the local church? Was it that way in the early church? Why is it that the pastor is the one who speaks every week? Should it be the responsibility of the pastor to prepare a sermon every week? Should the pastor expect the church to pay him a salary? Why do most pastors not work a regular job? Does going to Bible college make one a pastor? Why does the pastor seem to function in the same manner as fifty years ago? The internet has changed everything, so how can a pastor adapt in function? I think the answers can be found in how we define ministry. We tend to view a pastor as a position rather than what I believe is the true intention of ministry: **function**.

The fivefold ministry list is mentioned again in 1 Corinthians 12:27-28 and brings out the primary purpose of ministry: to build the body through the body as each member functions with the measure of grace given.

1 Corinthians 12:27-28, "Now **you** are the body of Christ, and **members** individually. And **God has appointed these in the church**; first apostles, second prophets, third teachers, after that miracles, then gifts of healings, helps, administrations, varieties of tongues." (NKJV)

Paul then points out that not all are apostles and etc. We can take away so many lessons here. These ministry gifts are drawn from the body itself. Remember this is the church Paul started when He met Aquila and Priscilla who were tent makers. This couple had a house church (Romans 16:3-5). It is therefore not a stretch to at least consider that some of these ministries became evident from the very members of the house churches.

Notice as well how this list is more expansive than the list in Ephesians. Paul clearly says that God has appointed miracles and gifts of healings to be **in** the church. This does not mean the grace gift of a pastor is not needed. It does seem to indicate that the pastor was not designed to have the prominent place in the church. This may be a completely new thought for many.

In fact, Paul clearly says in the body and in the church it is **first** apostles, **second** prophets. Evangelists produced miracles. Pastors are listed as helps and administrations. Prophets were more prominent than pastors. In fact, in Acts 13:1 it says there were certain prophets and teachers in the church at Antioch. Five people are specifically named. Notice it does not say pastors and teachers.

This would indicate that thirty years after Jesus died and resurrected, prophets still played a vital role in church life. Where did these prophets come from? The body. Where did they go to Bible college? What exactly did they teach? It is safe to conclude therefore that apostles were active in teaching, prophets were active in teaching, pastors were active in teaching. Evangelists were active in teaching, and it certainly is within reason to believe that some people were skilled at teaching, yet did not necessarily have any of the functions mentioned above.

I would suggest the working of miracles and the ability to heal the sick are tied to the evangelist as evidence of the gospel.

For example, Acts 21:8 Paul the Apostle travels to Caesarea and "went into the house of **Philip the Evangelist**, who was one of the seven first deacons, and (Paul) stayed with him (Philip)." Verse nine says Philip had four daughters who had the gift of prophecy. Acts 8:5-7, "Then **Philip** went down to the city of Samaria and preached Christ to them. And the **multitudes** with one accord heeded the things **spoken by Philip**, hearing and **seeing the miracles** which he did. For unclean spirits, crying with a loud voice, came out of many who were possessed; and

many who were paralyzed and lame were healed." (NKJV)

Philip the evangelist displayed miracles and healings just like Peter, Paul, and Jesus. We need to take notice of the context and subject matter of the entire chapter. The emphasis is on **the body** and the members of the body.

"But as it is God has placed and arranged the limbs and organs in the body, each one of them, just as He wished and saw fit with the best adaptation. But if the whole body were a single organ, where would the body be?" (AMP) 1 Corinthians 12:18

Paul compares the members of the church to a human body. The message conveyed is that ministry grace gifts are bestowed by God as He sees best for adaptation. This means that sometimes the very least of the church members are the ones God bestows these ministry gifts upon. We simply fail to discern this. We tend to rely on education for qualification.

What Is The Function Of A Pastor?

Romans Chapter 12 also talks about the body and ministry gifts. Take a fresh look at this chapter. Notice the emphasis on the **members** of the body and the emphasis on **function**. Apply this terminology to the pastor and all ministry. The Amplified Classic Version brings this out beautifully.

Romans 12:3-16, "For by the Grace of God given to me I warn everyone among you not to estimate and think of himself more highly than he ought [do not have an exaggerated opinion of **your own importance**], but to rate his ability with sober judgment, each according to the degree of faith **apportioned by God** to him. For as in one physical body we have many parts (organs, members) and all these parts do not have the same **function** or use. So we, as numerous as we are, are one body in Christ and individually we are parts one of another [mutually dependent on one another]. **Having gifts (faculties, talents, qualities) that differ according to the grace given us, let us use them**: [He whose gift is] prophecy [let him prophesy] according to the proportion of his faith; [He whose gift is] practical service, let him give himself to serving; He who teaches, in teaching; He who exhorts (encourages), to his exhortation; he who contributes, let him do it in simplicity and liberality; **he who gives aid and superintends**, with zeal and singleness of mind; he who does acts of mercy, with genuine cheerfulness and joyful eagerness.

[Let your] love be sincere (a real thing); hate what is evil, but hold fast to that which is good. Love one another with brotherly affection [as **members** of one family], giving precedence and showing honor to one another. Never lag in zeal and in earnest endeavor; be aglow and burning with the Spirit, serving the Lord.

Rejoice and exult in hope; be steadfast and patient in suffering and tribulation; be constant in prayer. Contribute to the needs of God's people [sharing in the necessities of the saints]; pursue the practice of hospitality. Bless those who persecute you [who are cruel in their attitude toward you]; bless and do not curse them. Rejoice with those who rejoice, and weep with those who weep. Live in harmony with one another, do not be haughty (snobbish, high minded, exclusive), but readily adjust yourself to [people, things] and give yourselves to humble tasks. Never overestimate yourself or be wise in your own conceits." (AMP)

Romans 12:18, "If possible, as far as it depends on you, live at peace with everyone."

The take away point here is that we are all the body, each one a member with various functions. This includes someone who is a pastor. The paradigm shift needed is to think of a pastor as a member function verses a position or rank. In fact, the text talks about someone who gives aid and superintends as being a member gift. An overseer as it were.

We can see the same description of this in the text from 1 Corinthians 12:28 where Paul lists administrations in the same list as apostles, prophets, and teachers. The word administration in the Greek gives the concept of being an aid and to attend to (superintend). The point is, the pastor was never designed to be the do all, be all and focal point. A thorough walk into the New Testament portrays the pastor in more of a facilitator role, helping to discern the gifting in the body. Someone who supports the body in specific functions. Someone who champions the call of God on each member of the body. Therefore a pastor needs to know the members in the body at a relational level. That means if church members ever become a calculated number that is needed to achieve the goal of the pastor, the function of a pastor has become corrupted. The grace gift of the pastor is misused and misguided by some who lack depth of understanding.

In fact, the early church lacked pastors or elders at first. We see in Acts 14:23 where Paul and Barnabas traveled to many cities and made many disciples (believers). Then they traveled back to those cities so **"when they had appointed elders** (pastors) in **every** church, and prayed with fasting, they commended them to the Lord in whom they had believed."

These elders did not attend a Bible college. It seems that praying with fasting to gain discernment as to who among the body truly had the grace gift of pastor was largely used as the determining factor. It is also within reason to believe relationships that were genuine also played a part. Think about it: what is the most often asked question when we visit a new church? Who is the pastor?! Most churches today would be lost without a pastor.

Paul gave this delegated responsibility of appointing elders to Titus. Titus 1:4-5, "To Titus, a true son in our common faith... For this reason I left you in Crete, that you should set in order the **things that are lacking**, and **appoint elders** (pastors) in every city as I commanded you." (NKJV)

Paul then goes on to list some qualifiers for a bishop/elder/pastor/overseer. So what can we learn here about the role and function of pastors? The churches were able to function without a pastor, but they realized something was lacking. There was a part of the body not fully functioning. Thus they appointed elders, or as we know it today, pastors. Imagine this dynamic of something lacking being applied to other ministries beside the pastor. Imagine a church with a pastor but lacking a prophet. Imagine a church with a pastor but lacking an apostle. Imagine a church with a pastor but lacking the ability to heal the sick and see genuine miracles happen in the church service. Not hard to imagine, all one needs to do is visit the average church anywhere and see this dynamic of missing functions evidenced.

These ministry gifts are needed just as much today as they were then. In fact, the Greek word *gifts* used here in Romans Chapter Twelve is the same Greek word used in First Corinthians Chapter Twelve. The Greek word is **charisma**. It means a spiritual endowment granted to an individual, a miraculous faculty, divine influence upon the heart. Thus all of these ministry gifts are simply that, divine gifting. We often miss the simplicity in this. Everyone enjoys a gift at Christmas time or to celebrate a birthday. The gift is given. We then determine how the gift will be used. The gift of apostle, prophet, pastor are sometimes misused. Sometimes people will see these gifts as something they are not.

1 Peter 5:1-3, "The **elders** who are among you I exhort, I am a fellow elder and a witness of the sufferings of Christ, and also a partaker of the glory that will be revealed. **Shepherd** the flock of God that is among you, **serving as overseers**, not by compulsion but willingly, not for dishonest gain but eagerly; nor as being **lords** over those entrusted to you, **but being examples** to the flock; and when the Chief Shepherd appears, you will receive the crown of glory that does not fade away." (NKJV)

The Greek word for *lord* means to exercise dominion over, subjugate, control. A pastor should carefully consider how this applies to daily interaction with others. God never designed for one person to dominate another. This applies to marriage and ministry. Many people today struggle with control issues. A pastor needs to address and resolve any such issues in his life before doing any kind of ministry.

We commonly define being an example to the church body as having an expected set of behaviors. A certain level of holiness if you will. This is usually only seen at church activities, but exactly how can a pastor be an example to the church body in very real and practical ways?

Break From The System

The most obvious way a pastor or elder can be an example to others is by having the evidence of the fruit of the spirit as listed in Galatians Chapter Five. That means when a pastor interacts with anyone, he needs to be loving, kind, patient, gentle, not involved in strife, and having self-control in all he does. This is ground level faith. Anyone can put on an act for an hour. This is a 24/7 lifestyle. No one should expect a pastor to be perfect and spot on all the time, but a pastor who can actually live this in front of people no matter where they are is truly being an example. I have seen pastors in grocery stores or getting gas who did not display this kind of good fruit. You never know who is watching, so again this must be a genuine lifestyle and not a pretense just for church.

This also needs to be applied **in** church. A pastor is often asked to pray for people. Personal prayer should be done with gentleness, kindness, patience, genuine love and compassion. A pastor who is short with someone, or even demanding is not being an example of what is good.

Paul used the illustration of a nursing mother to present a picture of the nurturing and gentle nature true ministry should look like.

1 Thessalonians 2:7-8, "But we were gentle among you, just as a nursing mother cherishes her own children. So affectionately longing for you, we were well pleased to impart to you not only the Gospel of

God, but also our own lives, because you had become dear to us." (NKJV)

A pastor would do well to cultivate a culture of independence. A church body that is dependent on the senior pastor and staff for everything tends to be stunted in becoming mature and effective. People are precious to Jesus the great shepherd. A pastor needs to value all people and not treat them as a number or an expendable asset. Too much micromanagement creates a system of control that can become dysfunctional.

The level of dependency the church body has upon a pastor can be seen by what the main focal point of the church service has become: the sermon. We worship. We pray. Yet what comprises most of the time spent is the message the pastor has prepared.

This may be a hard pill to swallow for some, but this format is no longer necessary and needs to change. The previous chapter on form and function provides some suggestions as to transitions and adaptations. It bears repeating that the internet has changed everything. A pastor no longer needs to spend hours and even days preparing a sermon. A pastor should always be diligent in study and prayer as would any dedicated believer.

There does need to be a transition from disseminating information to imparting inspiration, revelation and understanding. This needs to be done in a concise manner.

Is The Pastor The Only One Qualified To Speak?

This also begs the question, "Should the pastor be the only one to speak?" Also, does a speaker need to have attended a Bible college or be a certified minister? That depends on how you look at ministry. Do you see it as a position, or do you see it as a function? A pastor should be able to teach (1 Timothy 3:2). Yet each member of the body has something to share in the service including teaching as outlined in 1 Corinthians 14:26,

"What then is the right course, believers? When you meet together, **each one** has a psalm, **a teaching**, a revelation, a tongue, or an interpretation. Let everything be constructive and edifying and done for the good of all the church." (Amp)
1 Corinthians 14:26

Thus one does not need to have a degree in theology to speak in the public assembly. The size of the assembly would in large part determine the procedures and guidelines used. The pastor as well as any member of the body can utilize the internet to access all they need to be inspired and communicate the message to the end purpose that all be edified. That is not to say that reliance upon the Holy Spirit is diminished. Reliance upon the Spirit of God is primary in all situations. The point is, while formal education is good, it is not necessary to be effective in ministry. In fact the Apostle Paul considered all his formal learning to be refuse or garbage compared to the experiential knowledge of Jesus. (Philippians 3:8)

In many churches the pastor is the only one who speaks during every service. In light of all that is presented in this book, is this really necessary? Honestly, I have heard some pastors who are simply very poor at teaching. Yet they continue to teach. Why? Perhaps because of tradition. A transition as to the role of a pastor is very much needed. An upgrade if you will. The role of a pastor can be compared to a conductor of an orchestra. A conductor considers how each part fits in harmony. I would compare this to a concept called relational integration. Each instrument has a part to play. The composer of the piece (God) determines what notes are played by what instrument and also how they are played as well as how they flow with the other instruments. The conductor (Pastor) is merely the facilitator of the piece. The conductor does not actually perform the piece. The individual members of the orchestra (body) do the ministry. It becomes a beautiful sound. I suggest viewing videos of a conductor to get the mental picture of this concept.

Should A Pastor Be Paid A Salary By The Church?

Should a pastor depend on the church for a salary? Again that depends on how you view ministry. Recall from the chapter on tithe how the Apostle Paul worked to support himself. Paul and the others with him sometimes worked day and night so as to not be a financial burden on the church. Yet Paul also stated that they did have a right to be compensated for ministry. There is often the tendency to take such words literally and not consider the cultural context as well as the linguistic context. The first item to consider then is what type of ministry did Paul provide?

Paul did not merely teach the ancient scriptures, as it were. Paul imparted revelation and understanding of the Gospel of Grace such as no one else could. Paul was incredibly anointed to heal the sick, cast out demons, perform miracles and raise the dead! He was also heavily persecuted, beaten, imprisoned and traveled by foot through dangerous regions. Paul above anyone would have a right to be supported and compensated for ministry, yet many times he did not take advantage of this right. Many times he went hungry on purpose while waiting for basic necessities.

Compare this perspective of ministry to a pastor of today. What ministry is provided by a pastor of today? What kind of hardship does an average pastor endure? How many hours per day/week does a pastor spend in actual ministry? What is the average salary of a pastor? What modern opportunities exist in society for a pastor to earn money and yet still be effective in ministry?

This book is a framework for a true reformation. We cannot do step six until we do step one. Step one is to recognize we need to make changes. A pastor of a large church would naturally be bogged down with administrative priorities. In such cases that pastor could not do all that for free. That pastor may have a doctorate degree, spent years getting it, and be in major debt and have a family to support. Yet we need to curb the tide of doing this as the expected end. In other words, the goal need not be to spend years in Bible college in pursuit of growing a congregation and being paid $100,000 a year (that is the average salary of pastors who have a large church).

There is a recent trend to have a model of one church with many campuses. This has proven to be a more efficient use of funds. A recent study revealed that in most cases fifty percent of church funds are spent on administrative costs, including a salary for the pastor and staff. Yet even the many campus model tends to create an entitlement mentality for ministry. This needs to change. Giving is important. The church needs a safe and consistent place to meet. Heat, electricity and insurance is an expected expense. Yet imagine what the church at large could do to impact a nation if less money went to administration.

The United States alone has hundreds of thousands of churches. A shift in each church multiplied by that number of churches adds up to millions of dollars that can be better spent. The apostles often worked so as to be an example to others (see 2 Thessalonians 3:6-9). Think about it. A pastor may model all kinds of good virtues yet hard labor working in the real world tends not to be one. This is very important and should not be neglected. Verse ten of the above mentioned passage has the instruction that if anyone will not work, neither should they eat. Paul called this conduct disorderly. We somehow think that a pastor is exempt from this instruction. Some may say that being a pastor *is* the job and thus *is* work. Yet in this context Paul was most assuredly talking about labor. Paul worked as a tent maker. This is the kind of labor/work Paul was speaking of. Prayer, study, counseling, and speaking is not the kind of work defined here.

How can a pastor do both? Consider the time we live in. Consider the many opportunities that exist to earn money today as compared to just twenty years ago. A pastor can not only work as an employee but as a contractor as well. There are many opportunities in all kinds of fields, such as delivery, merchandising, instructors, network marketing and various service industries. All of these have flexible hours. Then of course there are many ways to work online performing many services. A pastor really needs to find ways to earn a living so as to be a genuine example to the church and the world.

Some scholars cite the following as a directive for a pastor to be paid. 1 Timothy 5:17, "The elders who direct the affairs of the church **well** are worthy of double honor, **especially** those whose work is preaching and teaching. For scripture says, "Do not muzzle an ox while it is treading out the grain," and "The worker deserves his wages." (NIV)

Notice that the primary purpose of an elder is administrative, elders who direct the affairs of the church. Then there are elders who preach and teach as well. It is quite evident that not all elders teach the word in the assembly. It is clear that an elder who can be an effective administrator **and** a persuasive communicator *is* a double honor; meaning they have two functions. This kind of person is deserving of pay. What kind of pay is prescribed? The ox was allowed to feed on the grain that was left over. The worker who deserves a wage is something Jesus said in Luke 10:7, "...Stay in that house, eating and drinking what they give you; for the laborer is worthy of his wages..."

The elders of that time who excelled were noticed. They went above and beyond expectations. Thus the Apostle Paul encouraged the church to share with them provisions such as food and lodging and perhaps other needs. These instructions to provide for elders who excel do not reflect a paid salary with perks such as we have today. It may also be deducted that elders who did not excel would not be provided for.

A pastor, above all else, needs to live in humility. This is lived out in many ways. The church body, like anything else, needs to have a sense of order. Yet too many times this order is manifested as rank and file.

Break From The System

The pastor is often viewed as a boss, even a demanding one. Yet when a pastor sees himself as holding a position or rank that is above others it creates an atmosphere of arrogance.

I relate a true story of how this presumed rank attitude is manifested. Many years ago, I called some local pastors about a project I felt passionate about. One pastor who called me back had an interesting way of relating to others. He answered by saying, "Hello, this is Pastor (Mike)". When I referred to him by his name alone, he would pause and say, "That's Reverend Mike." I believe He felt entitled to this **recognition of rank**. This was not a pastor of a large church. In fact it was a very small full gospel church out in the country.

Now another true story of a conversation I had with an international minister. This man has traveled in many countries, is well known and respected. He has quite a gift of teaching and healing. I called because I needed healing. He called me back. He said, "Hi, this is Dave." **Never once did he expect me to call him by a title**. This could be the very reason he is respected: **humility**. This may be a reason for the beautiful gifting: **humility.**

Identity for a pastor need not be defined by a title. Sadly this is typically the norm, for a pastor to be defined by the title. Imagine doing this with other aspects of life. For example, we never expect others to address us by the title of our occupation. We also do not typically use our occupation as our sole identity. There are a few exceptions, such as the President and

Congress, but other than the rare exceptions this is not the norm.

In fact, some people would be looked at as narcissistic if they went around and identified themselves by their occupation. Take time to picture what that conversation would sound like. Hello Teacher Mary, Hello Grocery Worker Tom, for example. How silly! Our identity is found in who we are in the heart of God. Our identity is in our **being**, not our doing. Our function is just that, a function. The expression of the Grace of God as He works with us and through us **is** our identity. We are all one body with many members and diverse functions. A pastor who insists on being addressed by title may come across to others as arrogant and even narcissistic.

A pastor is one part of the entire body. The pastor, the teacher, the prophet, the apostle, and the evangelist are all merely parts of the body who **serve** the body. The **function** is to equip the body so the body itself becomes ministers of the Grace of God that restores people to health (spirit, soul and body).

Chapter 5

The Challenge

Most churches today do not talk about or teach on subjects that they deem as non-essential. These topics tend to be Pentecostal and supernatural in nature. They are considered to be controversial and somewhat divisive. I am going to present a number of stories directly from the Bible. They are from the New Testament. They relate how Jesus interacted with people while on Earth. I will then present stories of how the Apostles and other followers of Jesus interacted with people after Jesus died and was also resurrected. These stories reveal the nature and purpose of Jesus. His Love. His passion. His mission. His compassion. His desire to see all people made whole.

Jesus Did What?

Acts 10:38, "How God anointed Jesus of Nazareth with the Holy Spirit and with power, who went about **doing good** and **healing all** who were oppressed by the devil, for God was with him."

Mark 6:56, "Wherever Jesus entered, into villages, cities, or the country, they laid the sick in the marketplaces, and begged Him that they might just touch the hem of His garment. And as many as touched Him were made well." (NKJV)

Luke 4:40, "Now when the sun was setting, all they who had any that were sick with divers diseases brought them unto Him (Jesus), and He laid hands on every one of them, and healed them."

Luke 6:17-19, "Jesus stood with a crowd of His disciples **and a great multitude of people** from all Judea and Jerusalem, and from the sea coast of Tyre and Sidon, who (the great multitude) came to hear Him (Jesus) and be healed of their diseases, as well as those who were tormented with unclean spirits. And they were healed. And the whole multitude sought to touch him (Jesus), **for power (virtue) went out from Him and healed them all**." (NKJV)

In Luke Chapter Seven, Jesus went to a town with the disciples along with a large crowd. Verse twelve records a dead man being carried out of the city gates. The man was in a coffin. The only child of his mother. She was also a widow. Verse thirteen, "When Jesus saw her He had **compassion** on her...then He came and touched the open coffin, and those who carried the coffin stood still. **Jesus said young man arise**. So he who was dead sat up and began to speak." (NKJV)

Matthew 10:1, "When Jesus called His twelve disciples, He gave them power over unclean spirits, to cast them out, and to heal all kinds of sickness and all kinds of disease." (NKJV)

Matthew 10:6-8, "...And as ye go, preach, saying, The kingdom of heaven is at hand. Heal the sick, cleanse the lepers, raise the dead, cast out demons. Freely ye have received, freely give."

Matthew 15:30-31, "And **great multitudes** came unto Him, having with them those that were lame, blind, dumb, maimed (crippled), and many others; and cast them down at His (Jesus) feet, **and He healed them**. Insomuch that the multitude wondered when they saw the mute speak, the maimed made whole, the lame to walk, and the blind to see; and they glorified the God of Israel."

The Apostles Did What?

We see in the second chapter of the book of Acts verses 1-4, there were 120 followers of Jesus in a room and they became filled with the Holy Spirit and experienced supernatural events. Peter spoke to the crowd that was gathered there. Acts 2:41 reports that many believed after Peter spoke. Three thousand people were added to the church community that day.

Acts 2:43, "**Many** signs and wonders were done **through** the apostles." The implication here is all twelve apostles did miracles, not just Peter. So where was Jesus? In Heaven. This is relevant because it displays the supernatural being done by ordinary humans who are connected to Jesus by and through the agency of the Holy Spirit!

Acts Chapter Three relates a story of a man who was completely crippled from birth. This man was placed at the gates outside the temple so he could beg for money. Acts 3:6-7 tells us that Peter and John spoke to the man and told him to rise up and walk, "Peter took him by the right hand and lifted him up, and **immediately his feet and ankle bones received strength**."

This man was forty years old. He not only walked into the temple with Peter and John, he was leaping and praising God. This was an extraordinary miracle because this man never walked during his entire life. There is simply no explanation as to how he had instant muscle and bone strength to walk and leap, let alone any coordination. All the people who saw this were filled with wonder and amazement! That day about five thousand people believed. Acts Chapter Four continues with the story.

The next day the rulers and other religious leaders were gathered together to address this miracle. These leaders perceived that Peter and John had been with Jesus because of the way they spoke, for they were uneducated and untrained men. We could learn much from this. Peter and John never went to Bible college.

They did not have a certificate of ordination. They were not associated with any religious organization. What qualified them? They knew Jesus and Jesus imparted to them wisdom, knowledge and spiritual power without the approval of men. Even the religious leaders were amazed.

They could not deny the insight into Jewish scripture nor the notable miracle that so many saw. The gathering of leaders did not like what was happening so they commanded the apostles to no longer speak about Jesus. How did the apostles respond? They prayed.

Acts 4:29-31, "Lord look upon their threatenings and grant at once to your bond slaves the ability to be speaking your word with all fearless confidence and freedom of speech while you stretch out your hand to heal, and grant that attesting miracles and miracles that arouse wonder may be done through the name of your holy servant Jesus. And having prayed, the place in which they were gathered was shaken..." (Kenneth S. Wuest).

Is this the prayer you and I pray? Do you hear this prayer being said in a public setting at your church? Does any pastor pray this during the message, and then believe for it to happen? If not, why not? We need to be humble and admit that what we are reading about is the real Jesus. This is who He is. This is what He does. Will the real Jesus stand up and be presented by us and our churches? We also know what motivated Jesus to heal people: Love and compassion. This should be our motivation as well.

Acts 5:12 **"And by the hands of the apostles were many signs and wonders wrought among the people."** The amplified version translates this as *miracles being continually done.*

Acts 5:14-16, "And believers were increasingly added to the Lord, **multitudes** of both men and women, so that they brought the sick out into the streets and laid them on beds and couches, that at least the shadow of Peter passing by might fall on some of them. Also a **multitude** had gathered from the surrounding cities to Jerusalem bringing sick people and those who were tormented by unclean spirits, **and they were all healed**." (NKJV)

We see later in this chapter that Peter and the other apostles were placed in prison again for doing those things the rulers told them not to do. Then an angel appears and talks to Peter and the others. The angel opens the prison doors and brings them out without being noticed. Peter and the others continued with speaking and healing and were once again arrested. This time they were put into a common prison, beaten and released again. So, we see a very real interaction between humans and an angelic being. What action did the apostles take after being in prison?

Break From The System

Acts 5:42, "And daily in the temple and in every house, they ceased not to teach and preach Jesus as the Christ."

Acts Chapter Six relates the story of deacons being chosen among the body of believers. These deacons were chosen to help with day to day service to the community in very practical ways. Stephen was one of these deacons.

Acts 6:8, "And Stephen full of faith and power, **did great wonders and miracles** among the people." Stephen was eventually stoned to death. There was a Pharisee named Saul who was present at this stoning. Saul actually held the outer garments of those doing the stoning so they could throw the stones without being encumbered by their clothing.

Acts 8:1-2, "Now Saul was consenting to his death. At that time a great persecution arose against the church at Jerusalem."

Acts 8:3, "As for Saul, he made havoc of the church, entering every house, and dragging off men and women, committing them to prison."

We could draw out many lessons from these events but for this chapter the background of Saul is most relevant. Acts Chapter Nine details the dramatic and supernatural conversion of Saul as he traveled on the road to Damascus. God worked amazing miracles through this man Saul *after* his conversion. We know him as the Apostle Paul.

There is another account of an ordinary person who saw healing and miracles happen as he prayed: Philip. Like Stephen, Philip was chosen to serve as a deacon. Yet we see Philip doing the same things that Peter, John, and Stephen did.

Acts 8:5-7, "Then Philip went down to the city of Samaria and preached Christ to them. And the **multitudes** with one accord heeded the things spoken by Philip, hearing and **seeing the miracles** which he did. For unclean spirits, crying with a loud voice, came out of many who were possessed; and **many who were paralyzed and lame were healed**." (NKJV)

We see further in Acts Chapter Eight a story of Simon the sorcerer. Acts 8:11, "People were attentive to Simon because for a long time he had amazed and dazzled them with his skill in magic arts." (NKJV) Yet because of Philip, Simon also became a believer in Jesus.

Acts 8:13, "So **Simon** followed Philip and **was amazed, seeing the miracles and signs** which were done through Philip." (NKJV)

This Philip could have been you or me. Philip was not a pastor. Philip was essentially a waiter! Philip was a believer. Acts 8:26, "**Now an angel of the Lord spoke to Philip**..." Pause and let that sink in.

Break From The System

Interaction with angels was a common event in the early church.

Philip went to the place the angel told him to go. Philip met a man who was a servant to a queen. Philip spoke to him about Jesus. The man believed and was baptized where they saw water.

Acts 8:39, "And when they were came up out of the water, the **Spirit of the Lord caught away Philip**...". The next verse says Philip was found in another city. Philip was caught away in one location and found in another.

Acts Chapter Nine details the conversion of Saul. This was no ordinary conversion by persuasion. Saul was on a road that led to Damascus, a city in Syria. Saul was on a mission to find and kill people who followed Jesus. On the way a light shone and blinded Saul. Then a voice spoke to him. The voice identified as Jesus. The others who traveled with Saul also heard the voice but saw no one. Now think about this, everyone heard the voice. A truly supernatural encounter with Jesus. Later in the chapter Saul begins to preach about Jesus.

Acts 9:33-35 tells yet another story about Peter. Peter heals a man who had been paralyzed for eight years. Acts 9:36-43 tells a different story about a woman named Tabitha who was a believer. She became sick and died. The Christians there wrapped Tabitha and placed her in an upper room. They heard that Peter was in a nearby town so they sent for him. The people who knew Tabitha were weeping. Peter knelt down and prayed and then said two words, "Tabitha arise!" The woman opened her eyes! Then she saw Peter and sat up! Wow!

Acts Chapter 14:1-10 (**Paul heals a crippled man, just like Peter**.) "Now it happened in Iconium that they went together to the synagogue of the Jews, and so spoke that a great multitude both of the Jews and of the Greeks believed. But the unbelieving Jews stirred up the Gentiles and poisoned their minds against the brethren. Therefore they stayed there a long time, speaking boldly in the Lord, who was bearing witness to the word of His grace, **granting signs and wonders to be done by their hands**. But the multitude of the city was divided: part sided with the Jews, and part with the apostles. And when a violent attempt was made by both the Gentiles and Jews, with their rulers, to abuse and stone them, they became aware of it and fled to Lystra and Derbe, cities of Lycaonia, and to the surrounding region. And they were preaching the gospel there. And in Lystra a certain man without strength in his feet was sitting, a cripple from his mother's womb, **who had never walked**. *This* man heard Paul speaking. Paul, observing him intently and seeing that he had faith to be healed, said with loud voice, "Stand up straight on your feet!" (NKJV)

The man leaped and walked. Notice that Paul was not alone. It says signs and wonders were done by **their** hands. The previous chapters tell us Paul was traveling with a party. The list includes Paul, Barnabas, Simeon, Lucius and Manaen. Acts 13:1 says these men were at the Church in Antioch and they were considered prophets and teachers. Notice it did not say pastors and teachers as we see in most of our churches today. It appears that prophets played a vital role in the church. This is something to think about.

God worked **unusual miracles** through Paul! Acts 19:11-12, "Now God worked unusual (and extraordinary) miracles by the hands of Paul, so that even handkerchiefs or towels or aprons which had touched His skin were carried away and placed on the sick, and diseases left them and evil spirits went out of them." (Amp)

What Should We Do?

James 5:16, "Confess your faults to one another, and pray for one another, that you may be healed..."

The Greek word used here for healed means to cure or make whole. Many times we pray for others from a distance because we are made aware of the need. Social media is a great vehicle for this use. This verse indicates a more intimate setting: face to face. The normal course in church ought to be to pray for one another to be healed while being face to face.

This time of personal prayer often produces a deeper experience and healing as well. People need all kinds of healing: physical healing is most obvious, yet healing of the soul (mind and emotions) is not so obvious but just as needed. Many people have deep wounds in the soul, thus quality time spent praying for someone face to face can create a beautiful vehicle for healing of the soul as well as the body.

The church should be a place where people learn various ways to do this. We can all pray for one another. We all have Jesus. We all have the Holy Spirit. We all have some measure of faith. We can have empathy and compassion for others. We can be kind, loving, patient and gentle when praying for others. We can all grow in faith and experience. We are all the body and yet each one of us have unique needs and unique spiritual gifting.

We seek doctors who can diagnose our problem and use specific treatments to hopefully find a cure. Sometimes this is done by surgical procedures. In like manner, we find in the Christian life spiritual gifts that enable the body to gain specific diagnosis and specific tools of healing for the repairs needed to be whole. Medical science does this as best as they can, and we should feel comfortable to use this when it serves us well. Yet we should also seek spiritual gifting that will benefit others. This is how the Apostle Paul and others were able to see many people healed and even miracles occur.

1 Corinthians 2:4, "And my speech and my preaching was not with enticing words of man's wisdom, but in **demonstration** of the Spirit and of power."

The Greek word for *demonstration* used here means to exhibit, show, demonstrate. We can all picture going to a museum to view various exhibits. Some exhibits are interactive. Paul did not merely speak the message but he demonstrated the reality of the message. How did he demonstrate the message? With demonstrations of the Spirit and power. The Gospel was not merely heard but also experienced.

The Greek word for *power* used here is *dunamis*. It means miraculous power, the ability to do a mighty work, a worker of a miracle. This is how Paul did church! Many churches today view this kind of spiritual demonstration as non-essential doctrine. Anyone can be saved without this kind of ministry being displayed, and anyone can have faith and live out Christian virtues without such demonstrations of healing and miracles. Yet, it seems obvious that the Apostle Paul did not view these things as non-essential.

There is a tendency to see the Apostle Paul as a one hit wonder. One person, one time, and that's it. Yet we have seen that many others did the same kind of demonstrations that Paul did to validate the message they preached. Validation is important in many areas of life. The message of salvation through Jesus is no less important. It is imperative that we see the message of the cross and the demonstration of the anointing of Jesus as both valid. We need both, the message and the demonstration.

Consider Hebrews 2:1-4, "We must pay the most careful attention, therefore, to what we have heard, so that we do not drift away. For since the **message** spoken through angels was binding, and every violation and disobedience received its just punishment, how shall we escape if we ignore so great a salvation? **This salvation**, which was first announced by the Lord, was confirmed to us by those who heard him. **God also testified to it by signs, wonders and various miracles**, and by gifts of the Holy Spirit distributed according to his will." (NIV)

This is worth reading in other translations, "So we must listen very carefully to the truths we have heard, or we may drift away from them. For since the messages from angels have always proved true and people have always been punished for disobeying them, what makes us think that we can escape if we are indifferent to this great salvation announced by the Lord Jesus himself and passed on to us by those who heard him speak. God has always shown us that these messages are true by signs and wonders and various miracles and by giving certain special abilities from the Holy Spirit to those who believe; yes, God has assigned such gifts to each of us." Hebrews 2:1-4 (TLB)

How Do We Get From Where We Are To Where They Were?

This is the challenge: to present the Gospel of Jesus with words **and** demonstrations of the Spirit that produce healing and miracles, as well as faith to believe that Jesus is very real. The writer of Hebrews, who many scholars believe was Paul, gives us a clue here as to how these demonstrations happened. Notice the implication, "by giving certain special abilities from the Holy Spirit. God has assigned **such gifts to each of us**."

The Apostle Paul talked about the gifts of the Spirit in 1 Corinthians 12:1-12, "Now concerning spiritual gifts, brethren, I would not have you ignorant. Ye know that ye were Gentiles, carried away unto these dumb idols, even as ye were led. Wherefore I give you to understand, that no man speaking by the Spirit of God calleth Jesus accursed: and that no man can say that Jesus is the Lord, but by the Holy Spirit. Now there are diversities of gifts, but the same Spirit. And there are diversities of administrations, but the same Lord. And there are diversities of operations, but it is the same God which works all in all. But the manifestation of the Spirit is given to every man to profit withal. For to one is given by the Spirit the word of wisdom; to another the word of knowledge by the same Spirit; To another faith by the same Spirit; To another the gifts of healings by the same Spirit; To another the working of miracles; To another prophecy; To another discerning of spirits;

To another diverse kinds of tongues; To another the interpretation of tongues; But all these worketh that one and the selfsame Spirit, dividing to every man severally as he will. For as the body is one, and hath many members, and all the members of that one body, being many, are one body; so also is Christ."

This is commonly known as the nine gifts of the Spirit. They originate from God and are given to the body of believers. Notice the emphasis on the members of the body. This indicates these spiritual demonstrations are not to be limited to the pastor, evangelist, or any other minister. These spiritual gifts are for them as well simply because they are members of the body. Any member of the body of believers can experience any of these spiritual gifts.

We are each unique therefore these gifts will operate in different ways with each member. Hence the verse that refers to diversities of operations and diversities of administrations. The members of the body are diverse, consequently the way these spiritual gifts are expressed through the members of the body will also tend to be diverse. There has been a trend in modern church life to present these gifts as natural abilities that are merely enhanced by God. Yet it is obvious the text calls them spiritual, not natural.

There is a translation by the scholar Kenneth S. Wuest that helps to bring out the richness of the Greek text.

Break From The System

1 Corinthians 12:1-12, "Now, concerning the spiritual gifts, brethren, I do not desire you to be ignorant. You all know that when you were Gentiles(non-Jews) you were led astray to the idols, which do not have the faculty of speech, as on different occasions you were led. Wherefore I make known to you that no individual speaking by means of God's Spirit says, Jesus is anathema{accursed}, and no person is able to say, Jesus is Lord, except by means of the Holy Spirit. Now, there are different distributions of spiritual gifts, these gifts being diverse from another, but there is the same Spirit. And there are different distributions of various kinds of ministries, but the same Lord. And there are different distributions of divine energy motivating these gifts in their operation, but the same God who by His divine energy operates them all in their sphere. But to each one there is constantly being given the clearly seen operations of the Spirit with a view to profit{of all}. For to one is given through the intermediate agency of the Spirit a word of wisdom, to another a word of knowledge according to the same Spirit, to another faith by the same Spirit, to another gifts of healing by the one Spirit, to another the working of miracles, to another the giving forth of divine revelations, to another the correct evaluation of those individuals who give forth divine revelations, and to another various kinds of languages, and to another the interpretation of languages. But all these the one and same Spirit is by divine energy putting into operation, dividing to each

one separately even as He desires. For even as the body is one and has many members, and all the members of the body being many, are one body, so also is The Christ." (Kenneth S. Wuest)

The Apostle Paul is simply illustrating that while the culture of that day had many idols (spirits), God has **one** Spirit. Idols cannot speak, but God does speak and makes Himself known by various gifts and demonstrations of the Holy Spirit. It is one Spirit but divided to the many members. This was a new concept for the people of that day and culture. Some believers were confused; they might have thought that as God works with and through many different people, there would be just as many spirits. Not so. There is one Spirit, one body, one Lord. Yet demonstrated in various ways and operations.

Notice here in the Wuest translation the emphasis on these gifts being imparted by divine energy. That would presuppose this is not natural energy. We could define it as divine energy which is spiritual in nature yet visible to the observer. Wuest points this out with the phrase, "clearly seen with a view."

Notice as well the limitations, **a word of wisdom**, **a word of knowledge**. It needs to be understood that while limited, this is not natural wisdom nor natural knowledge. It is a word that originates from the mind and heart of God sent to the believer through the agency of the Holy Spirit.

Some may like to think of it as a spiritual download into the heart and mind of the believer. The Holy Spirit is like a Wi-Fi signal secured and locked by Jesus. This word of wisdom, word of knowledge may be just one word or one phrase that only God would know. It is sent to demonstrate the reality of God. We can recall many stories of Jesus and the apostles demonstrating this kind of spiritual gifting. Take the time to reread those stories while looking for this particular spiritual gift within the story.

Notice further there are gifts of healing and working of miracles distributed to the members of the body. This includes you, me and the people who sit next to you in church. Therefore all qualify to receive these gifts.

I experienced some of these gifts from the very first day I was saved. I recall going to a church service that was very different from the Catholic service I had grown up with. People sang and raised their hands in worship. They prayed for one another and even spoke in tongues. That day I went from knowing about Jesus to actually knowing Him by experience. I was born anew. I was saved. Later that night before going to sleep I was thinking about how I felt and praying from my heart to God. Then I felt a warm heat flow through me from the inside out. Then almost by surprise I began to speak in tongues. The languages seemed to flow with ease. From that day on when I would meet people I would feel this intense warmth flow from inside me. I would pray for others and sometimes they would feel this intense warmth flow to them. Some of them experienced a healing. This was my discovery of the gifts of healing and of tongues.

As time passed and I grew in maturity, I would begin to experience the word of knowledge. That is, I would meet someone new in church or in the market place and I could perceive a specific point in the body where they were experiencing pain, even though they never told me. God downloaded information to me by the Holy Spirit that was not known by natural means. They would acknowledge that this information was indeed correct. I would ask them if I could pray for them. Most said yes, some said no, some were a bit freaked out. When I prayed, this heat would flow from me to them and in many cases they were healed. This was my discovery of the gift of word of knowledge and gifts of healing working together to produce faith, hope and healing in people.

I learned that these gifts are real and are valid for today. Some may make a theological argument against this. I think we need to make an honest evaluation that perhaps we have been infected with bad theology. This is part of the challenge: To adjust our doctrinal stance so that God may express Himself through His body. We need to place ourselves in a receptive mode and de-clutter our theology so we can have the capacity for spiritual download.

The term for a spiritual download used in the Bible is called impartation.

Romans 1:11, "For I long to see you, that I may impart unto you some spiritual gift, to the end that you may be established."

The Apostle Paul wanted to visit the church in Rome that he may impart some **spiritual** gift. The Greek word for *spiritual* means divine, non-human, supernatural, spiritual. Notice as well that here Paul indicates **he** could impart spiritual gifts. This may be a strange concept for some to believe, yet we can all see these gifts are not natural gifts. The Greek word *gift* here is *charisma*. It means divine, spiritual endowment, miraculous faculty. This seems to be a motivating factor for Paul to visit various churches. To impart spiritual and divine endowment that he had received from God in order that the individual members may be *established*. The Wuest translation uses the word *stabilized*. These spiritual gifts Paul refers to are likely to be the same spiritual gifts Paul wrote about in Corinthians. It would seem that this expression of ministry is a missing link in the current church structure. There are many qualified speakers who visit churches and do impart encouragement, knowledge, hope, faith and such virtues. This is good and needed, yet it is my hope that many will read this and have an epiphany.

True spiritual and supernatural gifting is filled with love, beauty and wonder. It is lacking in most churches. Some that claim to have it often mistake emotionalism and fanaticism for the genuine. I relate a true personal story which illustrates just how practical and needed genuine spiritual gifting can be. I was in my early forties and working a very physical job. I pulled a muscle in my back while loading my truck. I went to a doctor who prescribed rest and medication, but I found no relief. I had to return to work due to my contract status. I needed a healing and fast, so I called someone who traveled in ministry and has a genuine gift of healing. This person was about a thousand miles away yet within minutes of praying over the phone my back loosened up and the pain was gone. I was instantly healed and went to work that day with no further problems!

This real life story perfectly illustrates the concept and reality of impartation. One member of the body, who happened to be in ministry, imparting to another member of the body a spiritual gift that produced a healing to the benefit of many. This was done without emotionalism, without some big dramatic scene, outside the four walls of the church, and without the exchange of money. A perfect picture of how the church and the church body should function every week, every day, and everywhere.

What should we do? Start doing something. Take action. Start with James 5:16. Pray for one another with the intention of being healed and being made whole. Take baby steps. Expect and allow God to work with and through all of the body! It has been said that whatever we focus on is where we will end up. This is true in many ways. It would behoove us to focus less on the pastor and more on the body. The Apostle Paul actually encouraged the early church to desire and pursue spiritual gifting.

1 Corinthians 14:1, "Follow the way of Love and eagerly desire gifts of the Spirit, especially prophecy." (NIV)

Anyone would agree with the first five words of this verse, follow the way of love, and we should absolutely do this with all diligence and behavior. So it would be wise to follow the last nine words of this verse as well. Years ago I heard a saying that has stuck with me, "When was the last time you did something for the first time?" This is part of the challenge as well, do something you have not done before. Take a few concepts presented in this book and begin to implement them. Step by step. Keep at it until you see results.

Chapter 6

A Bell, A Pomegranate, And The Church

Exodus 28:31-35, "Make the robe of the ephod entirely of blue cloth, with an opening for the head in its center. There shall be a woven edge like a collar around this opening, so that it will not tear. Make pomegranates of blue, purple and scarlet yarn around the hem of the robe, with gold bells between them. The gold bells and the pomegranates are to alternate around the hem of the robe. Aaron must wear it when he ministers. The sound of the bells will be heard when he enters the Holy Place before the Lord and when he comes out, so that he will not die." (NIV)

This is a beautiful picture of ministry. This may be from the Old Testament yet we can relate this to the New Testament. Old Testament concealed, New Testament revealed! This passage is rich in practical lessons about everyday ground level ministering to people. Aaron was made a priest. Today **we** are a chosen generation and a royal priesthood (1 Peter 2:9) because of Jesus.

Aaron wore specific garments with specific colors. These colors represent something for us today and give us a picture of our identity in God. **Blue** represents heaven or a heavenly atmosphere. This robe was entirely of blue.

Isaiah 61:10, "I delight greatly in the Lord; my soul rejoices in my God. For he has **clothed me** with garments of **salvation** and arrayed me in a **robe** of his righteousness, as a bridegroom adorns his head **like a priest**, and as a bride adorns herself with jewels." (NIV)

Galatians 3:27, "For all of you who were baptized into Christ have **clothed** yourselves with Christ." (NASB)

We can think of it this way; we are all clothed with heaven because Jesus came from heaven and we are one with him. The lesson here is to become aware of the heavenly atmosphere we carry when we speak to people and pray for them.

The color purple speaks of royalty. Jesus is King of Kings and Lord of Lords (1 Timothy 6:15). And because of Jesus **we** are a royal priesthood (1 Peter 2:9).

The color of scarlet speaks of the forgiveness granted when Jesus gave his innocent blood on the cross. The yarn along the hem of the garment was made to look like a fruit, a pomegranate. The placement of this spiritual fruit along the hem is very intentional. **It is where heaven meets earth**.

The gold bells were also to be placed on the hem. Gold has value and represents Glory and the purity of God. Bells make a sound. These bells represent the various spiritual gifts mentioned in previous chapters.

The bells and the pomegranates were to alternate all along the hem. A bell and a pomegranate. **A bell and a pomegranate**. The lesson applied here is today we have spiritual gifts **and** spiritual fruits. The Apostle Paul listed both categories in such a fashion as to have nine spiritual gifts and nine spiritual fruits. The lists are found in 1 Corinthians 12:1-11 and Galatians 5:22, respectively. Both are needed to be effective. Both are gifts provided by God and expected attire to be clothed with. It is also expected that we should be clothed with humility (1 Peter 5:5). When all of these virtues are incorporated into daily life and blended to work together, they create a beautiful sound and atmosphere. This is why the Apostle Paul wrote the following about the fruit of Love;

1 Corinthians 13:1, "Though I speak with the tongues of men and angels, and have not love, I have become sounding brass or a clanging cymbal." (NKJV)

We can imagine what it would sound like when Aaron walked around if he only had bells clanging against each other. It is certainly possible and even probable that Paul being a Jewish scholar would be thinking of the story of Aaron when he wrote to these new believers in Jesus.

Again Paul wrote the same idea, 1 Corinthians 14:1, "**Follow the way of Love and eagerly desire gifts of the Spirit**, especially prophecy." (NIV)

Galatians 5:22, "The Fruit of the spirit is <u>Love, Joy, Peace, Patience, Kindness, Goodness, Faithfulness, Gentleness, Self-Control</u>." This is the nature of spiritual fruit. It is worth noting that the Greek word here for fruit is *karpos*. It means fruit that is fully ripe, plucked, pulled off, taken, ready to eat. Hence, this spiritual fruit is mature. So go over that list again and think about each one being fully mature in your life. Imagine what each one would feel like. The importance of each and every one of these spiritual virtues cannot be emphasized enough. Imagine the impact this will produce with all relationships. Imagine the impact this will produce in ministry. Imagine creating an atmosphere of peace rather than strife. What does that look like? How does that feel? Picture praying for others with an atmosphere of peace, gentleness, kindness and self-control.

Many years ago when I was new in the faith I would observe ministers preaching and praying for people with great drama and emotionalism. I observed ministers exercising the gifts of the spirit, yet not being patient, gentle or kind with people. I learned by observation what not to do. I learned that we desperately need what I call *"fruit wrapped gifting."* The ability to wrap everything we do in spiritual fruit creates a beautiful life and sound that others will notice. This can dramatically change the dynamics of a marriage. This can dramatically change work place dynamics. This definitely will make church life and ministry better if we all start to do this as a daily practice. It is a process.

We can all start by being aware that in Heaven there is no fear, only courage. No anger, only Love. No fighting and arguing, only peace. No strife, only patience and gentleness. As we go through our day we can make an effort to be aware of what virtues are flowing through us in the moment.

Is Love flowing or anger? Is Grace flowing or judgment and condemnation? Is peace flowing like a river or are we living in strife? Is stability flowing or chaos and self-created crisis? Objectively evaluate your life. Ask for input from others. We can then make adjustments on the spot by exerting self-control and patience. This is a very good exercise in the life skill of awareness. The fruit we produce in our life will be seen by others.

We will no longer feel a compulsion to sell the fruit of the Gospel when people can taste and see the goodness of God working through us. We will no longer study the Bible for knowledge, rather we will study to become *fruit wrapped gifting* for others.

CONCLUSION

Ephesians 2:19-22, "So then you are no longer strangers and aliens, but you are fellow citizens with the saints, and are of God's household, having been built on the foundation of the apostles and prophets, Christ Jesus himself being the chief cornerstone, in whom the whole building, being fitted together, is growing into a holy temple in the Lord, in whom you are also being built together into a dwelling of God in the Spirit." (NASB)

The foundation of any church should follow the blueprint laid out by those who started it. We have examined how Jesus did life and church. We have looked at how the apostles and prophets did church. The upward structures may evolve over time yet the foundation needs to be duplicated and maintained.

1 Corinthians 3:10-11, "According to the grace of God given to me, I as a skillful master builder laid a foundation, but another builds upon it. But let each one be taking heed **how** he builds upon it, for an alternative foundation no one is able to lay alongside of the one which is being laid, which foundation is a person, Jesus Christ." (Kenneth S. Wuest)

The subtitle of this book is: perspectives on **how** we do church. Paul admonishes the church then and future readers to take heed as to the foundation and as to how we build upon it. My maternal grandfather was a brick layer. He built a number of houses one brick at a time. He was skilled at his trade. We, the church body, are living stones who are being built up as a spiritual house (1 Peter 2:5). Let us value each stone as we build this spiritual house one brick at a time. Let us ensure we have great skill in so doing. Let us build it with spiritual tools. 2 Corinthians 3:6, "He has made us competent ministers of a new covenant-not of the letter but of the Spirit; for the letter kills but the Spirit gives life." (NIV)

A church that ministers from a posture of obedience to the letter will create more divisiveness than a church that ministers from a posture of grace. The tendency in most people is to claim we are right and others are wrong. Paul often addressed divisiveness within the church body. He poised a question in 1 Corinthians 1:13, "Is Christ divided?" The answer is obvious. Consequently that would mean his body should also not be divided. 1 Corinthians 12:25, "That there should be no *schism* in the body; but that the members should have the same care for one another." The dictionary defines *schism* as a division, discord, disharmony usually caused by differences in opinions or beliefs.

1 Corinthians 1:10-11, "I beg of you, please, that all of you be speaking the same thing, and that there be

no factions among you, but that the breaches in your fellowship caused by these factions having been healed, you may remain perfectly united in the sphere of the same mind and in the sphere of the same opinion. For it was made clear to me concerning you, my brethren, by members of Chloe's household, that there are wranglings among you". (Kenneth S. Wuest)

We know that cracks can occur in the foundations of a building. This can cause serious structural damage if not properly fixed. The fix needed in some churches will require change. Change is sometimes difficult, as we tend to be creatures of habit. There is a need to change the way we think about change. Change is often resisted. Humility accepts change as a natural progression toward a goal. Here are some goals I suggest.

- Do not be satisfied with the status quo.
- To expect the whole pizza and not one with slices missing.
- To have church not be so-so, i.e. same old, same old.
- To think of church as chairs facing each other rather than chairs next to each other and facing forward.
- To experience more than just a sermon when we gather.
- To make church a place for spiritual impartation as well as information.

- ➤ To bring all believers into maturity in God so they are equipped to do anything the Gospel teaches them to do.
- ➤ To make a transition concerning the weekly collection of money.

The intent of church offerings is prescribed in 1 Corinthians 16:1-2, "Now concerning the collection for the **saints** as I have given order to the churches of Galatia, even so do ye. Upon the first day of the week let every one of you lay by him in store, **as** God hath prospered him, that there be no gatherings when I come." (NASB)

It is understood that a church has bills to pay, yet we can clearly see the weekly collection was to be set aside for the less fortunate members of the community. This is a noble goal.

Pastors need to see that being a pastor is a function rather than a profession. Church leaders need to view themselves as facilitators who encourage believers to be independent thinkers. Church leaders would be better leaders if they began to teach people **how** to think about the Bible, not what to think. Church leaders need to practice humility. In fact all of us need to practice true humility. We are all representatives of Jesus on earth. Each one having a unique function and mission. Our overall mission is to love the world and each other. Our task is not to make others conform to our beliefs rather it is to attract others to the saving beauty of Jesus so that they become **his** disciple.

The traditional church is often thought of as denominational. The contemporary churches are often identified as non-denominational. The contemporary church has, in many ways, become the new traditional church. What do I mean by that? Simply this: every new church looks just like every other new church. Many people talk about the need for revival, and we should consider the need for a reformation as well. The focus is clear, it is all about a person, Jesus the anointed one.

John 10:27, "My sheep hear my voice, and I know them, and they follow me." (NKJV)

This may very well be the ultimate goal, to be able to hear the voice of Jesus and follow him. To follow Jesus as a sheep would follow a shepherd. That means to recognize his face, his presence, the sound of his voice and then walk in the direction he walks.

Religion is often associated with following a set of commands. The ability to follow the great shepherd without needing a command is to truly know him. How amazing would it be if we were able to bring others to this place of knowing the great shepherd, Jesus. They would no longer need the church to be a babysitter. The way we do church would change. May we begin to seek and find better ways to accomplish this ultimate goal.

John 10:27, "My sheep hear my voice, and I know them, and they follow me." (NKJV)

Kenneth E. Purcell

About the Author

Kenneth E. Purcell was born in 1963. He married his wife, Wendy Purcell in 1989. They have two sons, David and Stephen. Ken was born into an Irish and Italian family. He was raised as a Roman Catholic. At age seventeen he experienced the overwhelming love of God and went from hearing of Jesus to truly knowing him. Thus began a lifelong journey of faith. He is a gifted musician and percussionist. Ken draws on thirty-five years of experience and study to present perspectives that are interesting and enlightening. He is also the founder of Practical Faith Institute on social media.

Contact Info: kenneth.e.purcell@gmail.com

Break From The System

Reader's Notes

For more in depth study, The NarrowPath.com is a great resource for lecture series on church history.

Made in the USA
Columbia, SC
07 May 2018